THE INQUISITION

A CRITICAL AND HISTORICAL
STUDY OF THE COERCIVE
POWER OF THE CHURCH

BY

E. VACANDARD

TRANSLATED FROM THE SECOND EDITION BY
BERTRAND L. CONWAY, C.S.P.

Catholic Authors Press
Hartford, 2006

Nihil Obstat:

    THOMAS J. SHAHAN, S.T.D.

Imprimatur:

    ✠ JOHN M. FARLEY, D.D.,
       Archbishop of New York.

NEW YORK, June 24, 1907.

The Inquisition, a Critical and Historical Study of the Coercive Power of the Church
Copyright © 1907 Bertrand L. Conway
New elements
copyright 2006 Catholic Authors Press
All rights reserved

ISBN: 978-0-9789432-1-9

Printed in the United States of America

Catholic Authors Press
www.CatholicAuthors.org

PREFACE

THERE are very few Catholic apologists who feel inclined to boast of the annals of the Inquisition. The boldest of them defend this institution against the attacks of modern liberalism, as if they distrusted the force of their own arguments. Indeed they have hardly answered the first objection of their opponents, when they instantly endeavor to prove that the Protestant and Rationalistic critics of the Inquisition have themselves been guilty of heinous crimes. "Why," they ask, "do you denounce our Inquisition, when you are responsible for Inquisitions of your own?"

No good can be accomplished by such a false method of reasoning. It seems practically to admit that the cause of the Church cannot be defended. The accusation of wrong-doing made against the enemies they are trying to reduce to silence comes back with equal force against the friends they are trying to defend.

It does not follow that because the Inquisition of Calvin and the French Revolutionists merits the reprobation of mankind, the Inquisition of the Catholic Church must needs escape all censure. On the contrary, the unfortunate comparison made between them naturally leads one to think that both deserve equal blame. To our mind, there is only one way of defending the attitude of the Catholic Church in the Middle

Ages toward the Inquisition. We must examine and judge this institution objectively, from the standpoint of morality, justice, and religion, instead of comparing its excesses with the blameworthy actions of other tribunals.

No historian worthy of the name has as yet undertaken to treat the Inquisition from this objective standpoint. In the seventeenth century, a scholarly priest, Jacques Marsollier, canon of the Uzès, published at Cologne (Paris), in 1693, a *Histoire de l'Inquisition et de son Origine*. But his work, as a critic has pointed out, is "not so much a history of the Inquisition, as a thesis written with a strong Gallican bias, which details with evident delight the cruelties of the Holy Office." The illustrations are taken from Philip Limborch's *Historia Inquisitionis*.[1]

Henry Charles Lea, already known by his other works on religious history, published in New York, in 1888, three large volumes entitled *A History of the Inquisition of the Middle Ages*. This work has received as a rule a most flattering reception at the hands of the European press, and has been translated into French.[2] One can say without exaggeration that it is "the most extensive, the most profound, and the most thorough history of the Inquisition that we possess."[3]

It is far, however, from being the last word of historical criticism. And I am not speaking here of

[1] Paul Fredericq, *Historiographie de l'Inquisition*, p. xiv. Introduction to the French translation of Lea's book on the Inquisition.

[2] *Histoire de l'Inquisition au moyen âge*, Salomon Reinach. Paris, Fischbacher, 1900–1903.

[3] Paul Fredericq, *loc. cit.*, p. xxiv.

the changes in detail that may result from the discovery of new documents. We have plenty of material at hand to enable us to form an accurate notion of the institution itself. Lea's judgment, despite evident signs of intellectual honesty, is not to be trusted. Honest he may be, but impartial never. His pen too often gives way to his prejudices and his hatred of the Catholic Church. His critical judgment is sometimes gravely at fault.[1]

Tanon, the president of the Court of Cassation, has proved far more impartial in his *Histoire des Tribunaux de l'Inquisition en France*.[2] This is evidently the work of a scholar, who possesses a very wide and accurate grasp of ecclesiastical legislation. He is deeply versed in the secrets of both the canon and the civil law. However, we must remember that his scope is limited. He has of set purpose omitted everything that happened outside of France. Besides he is more concerned with the legal than with the theological aspect of the Inquisition.

On the whole, the history of the Inquisition is still to be written. It is not our purpose to attempt it; our ambition is more modest. But we wish to picture this institution in its historical setting, to show how it originated, and especially to indicate its relation to the Church's notion of the coercive power prevalent in the Middle Ages. For, as Lea himself says: " The Inquisition was not an organization arbitrarily devised and imposed upon the judicial system of Christendom by the ambition or fanaticism of the Church. It was

[1] The reader may gather our estimate of this work from the various criticisms we will pass upon it in the course of this study.
[2] Paris, 1893.

rather a natural—one may almost say an inevitable—evolution of the forces at work in the thirteenth century, and no one can rightly appreciate the process of its development and the results of its activity, without a somewhat minute consideration of the factors controlling the minds and souls of men during the ages which laid the foundation of modern civilization."[1]

We must also go back further than the thirteenth century and ascertain how the coercive power which the Church finally confided to the Inquisition developed from the beginning. Such is the purpose of the present work. It is both a critical and an historical study. We intend to record first everything that relates to the suppression of heresy, from the origin of Christianity up to the Renaissance; then we will see whether the attitude of the Church toward heretics can not only be explained, but defended.

We undertake this study in a spirit of absolute honesty and sincerity. The subject is undoubtedly a most delicate one. But no consideration whatever should prevent our studying it from every possible viewpoint. Cardinal Newman, in his Historical Sketches, speaks of "that endemic perennial fidget which possesses certain historians about giving scandal. Facts are omitted in great histories, or glosses are put upon memorable acts, because they are thought not edifying, whereas of all scandals such omissions, such glosses, are the greatest."[2]

A Catholic apologist fails in his duty to-day if he writes merely to edify the faithful. Granting that the history of the Inquisition will reveal things we never

[1] Preface, p. iii. [2] Vol. ii, p. 231.

dreamed of, our prejudices must not prevent an honest facing of the facts. We ought to dread nothing more than the reproach that we are afraid of the truth. "We can understand," says Yves Le Querdec,[1] " why our forefathers did not wish to disturb men's minds by placing before them certain questions. I believe they were wrong, for all questions that can be presented will necessarily be presented some day or other. If they are not presented fairly by those who possess the true solution, or who honestly look for it, they will be by their enemies. For this reason we think that not only honesty but good policy require us to tell the world all the facts. . . .Everything has been said, or will be said some day. . . . What the friends of the Church will not mention will be spread broadcast by her enemies. And they will make such an outcry over their discovery, that their words will reach the most remote corners and penetrate the deafest ears. We ought not to be afraid to-day of the light of truth; but fear rather the darkness of lies and errors."

In a word, the best method of apologetics is to tell the whole truth. In our mind, apologetics and history are two sisters, with the same device: "*Ne quid falsi audeat, ne quid veri non audeat historia.*"[2]

[1] *Univers*, June 2, 1906.   [2] Cicero, De Oratore ii, 15.

CONTENTS

PREFACE..

CHAPTER I

FIRST PERIOD (I–IV CENTURY): THE EPOCH OF THE PERSECUTIONS.

The Teaching of St. Paul on the Suppression of Heretics.
The Teaching of Tertullian........................
The Teaching of Origen...........................
The Teaching of St. Cyprian......................
The Teaching of Lactantius ....
Constantine, Bishop in Externals..................
The Teaching of St. Hilary........................

CHAPTER II

SECOND PERIOD (FROM VALENTINIAN I TO THEODOSIUS II). THE CHURCH AND THE CRIMINAL CODE OF THE CHRISTIAN EMPERORS AGAINST HERESY.

Imperial Legislation against Heresy................
The Attitude of St. Augustine towards the Manicheans.
St. Augustine and Donatism......................
The Church and the Priscillianists.................
The Early Fathers and the Death Penalty...........

CHAPTER III

THIRD PERIOD (A.D. 1100–1250). THE REVIVAL OF THE MANICHEAN HERESIES.

Adoptianism and Predestinationism.................
The Manicheans in the West......................
Peter of Bruys...................................
Henry of Lausanne...............................

CONTENTS

	PAGE
Arnold of Brescia	30
Éon de l'Étoile	31
Views of this Epoch upon the Suppression of Heresy	32

CHAPTER IV

FOURTH PERIOD (FROM GRATIAN TO INNOCENT III). THE INFLUENCE OF THE CANON LAW, AND THE REVIVAL OF THE ROMAN LAW.

Executions of Heretics	39
The Death Penalty for Heretics	41
Legislation of Popes Alexander III and Lucius III and Frederic Barbarossa against Heretics	43
Legislation of Innocent III	43
The First Canonists	64

CHAPTER V

THE CATHARAN OR ALBIGENSIAN HERESY: ITS ANTI-CATHOLIC AND ANTI-SOCIAL CHARACTER.

The Origin of the Catharan Heresy	50
Its Progress	51
It Attacks the Hierarchy, Dogmas, and Worship of the Catholic Church	52
It Undermines the Authority of the State	56
The Hierarchy of the Cathari	58
The *Convenenza*	59
The Initiation into the Sect	60
Their Customs	63
Their Horror of Marriage	66
The *Endura* or Suicide	70

CHAPTER VI

FIFTH PERIOD (GREGORY IX AND FREDERIC II). THE ESTABLISHMENT OF THE MONASTIC INQUISITION.

Louis VIII and Louis IX	75
Legislation of Frederic II against Heretics	76
Gregory IX Abandons Heretics to the Secular Arm	78
The Establishment of the Inquisition	83

CHAPTER VII

SIXTH PERIOD. DEVELOPMENT OF THE INQUISITION. (INNOCENT IV AND THE USE OF TORTURE.)

	PAGE
The Monastic and the Episcopal Inquisitions	97
Experts to Aid the Inquisitors	99
Ecclesiastical Penalties	101
The Infliction of the Death Penalty	103
The Introduction of Torture	106

CHAPTER VIII

THEOLOGIANS, CANONISTS AND CASUISTS.

Heresy and Crimes Subject to the Inquisition	115
The Procedure	119
The Use of Torture	121
Theologians Defend the Death Penalty for Heresy	123
Canonists Defend the Use of the Stake	128
The Church's Responsibility in Inflicting the Death Penalty	128

CHAPTER IX

THE INQUISITION IN OPERATION.

Its Field of Action	132
The Excessive Cruelty of Inquisitors	133
The Penalty of Imprisonment	137
The Number of Heretics Handed Over to the Secular Arm	143
Confiscation	147
The *auto-da-fé*	150

CHAPTER X

CRITICISM OF THE THEORY AND PRACTICE OF THE INQUISITION.

Development of the Theory on the Coercive Power of the Church	152
Intolerance of the People	155
Intolerance of Sovereigns	156

CONTENTS

	PAGE
The Church and Intolerance	158
The Theologians and Intolerance	158
Appeal to the Old Testament	159
England and the Suppression of Heresy	160
The Calvinists and the Suppression of Heresy	163
Cruelty of the Criminal Code in the Middle Ages	165
The Spirit of the Age Explains the Cruelty of the Inquisition	166
Defects in the Procedure	167
Abuses of Antecedent Imprisonment and Torture	169
Heretics who were also Criminals	170
Heresy Punished as Such	172
Should the Death Penalty be Inflicted upon Heretics?	174
The Responsibility of the Church	177
Abuses of the Penalties of Confiscation and Exile	179
The Penitential Character of Imprisonment	182
The Syllabus and the Coercive Power of the Church	182
INDEX	189

THE INQUISITION

CHAPTER I

FIRST PERIOD

I-IV Century

The Epoch of the Persecutions

St. Paul was the first to pronounce a sentence of condemnation upon heretics. In his Epistle to Timothy, he writes: " Of whom is Hymeneus and Alexander, whom I have delivered up to Satan, that they may learn not to blaspheme." [1] The Apostle is evidently influenced in his action by the Gospel. The one-time Pharisee no longer dreams of punishing the guilty with the severity of the Mosaic Law. The death penalty of stoning, which apostates merited under the old dispensation,[2] has been changed into a purely spiritual penalty: excommunication.

---

[1] I Tim. i. 20. Cf. Tit. iii. 10–11. " A man that is a heretic, after the first and second admonition, avoid, knowing that he, that is such an one, is subverted, and sinneth, being condemned by his own judgment."

[2] Deut. xiii. 6–9; xvii. 1–6.

During the first three centuries, as long as the era of persecution lasted, the early Christians never thought of using any force save the force of argument to win back their dissident brethren. This is the meaning of that obscure passage in the *Adversus Gnosticos* of Tertullian, in which he speaks of "driving heretics (*i.e.*, by argument), to their duty, instead of trying to win them, for obstinacy must be conquered, not coaxed." [1] In this work he is trying to convince the Gnostics of their errors from various passages in the Old Testament. But he never invokes the death penalty against them. On the contrary, he declares that no practical Christian can be an executioner or jailer. He even goes so far as to deny the right of any disciple of Christ to serve in the army, at least as an officer, "because the duty of a military commander comprises the right to sit in judgment upon a man's life, to condemn, to put in chains, to imprison and to torture." [2]

If a Christian has no right to use physical force, even in the name of the State, he is all the more bound not to use it against his dissenting brethren in the name of the Gospel, which is a law of gentleness. Tertullian was a Montanist when he wrote this. But although he wrote most bitterly against the Gnostics whom he detested, he always protested against the use of brute force in the matter of religion. "It is a fundamental human right," he says, "a privilege of nature, that every man should worship according to his convictions. It is assuredly no part of religion to

---

[1] *Adversus Gnosticos Scorpiace*, cap. ii, Migne, P. L., vol. ii, col. 125.

[2] *De Idololatria*, cap. xvii, P. L., vol. i, col. 687.

compel religion. It must be embraced freely, and not forced."¹ These words prove that Tertullian was a strong advocate of absolute toleration.

Origen likewise never granted Christians the right to punish those who denied the Gospel. In answering Celsus, who had brought forward certain texts of the Old Testament that decreed the death penalty for apostasy, he says: "If we must refer briefly to the difference between the law given to the Jews of old by Moses, and the law laid down by Christ for Christians, we would state that it is impossible to harmonize the legislation of Moses, taken literally, with the calling of the Gentiles. . . . For Christians cannot slay their enemies, or condemn, as Moses commanded, the contemners of the law to be put to death by burning or stoning."²

St. Cyprian also repudiates in the name of the Gospel the laws of the Old Testament on this point. He writes as follows: "God commanded that those who did not obey his priests or hearken to his judges,³ appointed for the time, should be slain. Then indeed they were slain with the sword, while the circumcision of the flesh was yet in force; but now that circumcision has begun to be of the spirit among God's faithful servants, the proud and contumacious are slain with the sword of the spirit by being cast out of the Church."⁴

The Bishop of Carthage, who was greatly troubled by stubborn schismatics, and men who violated every

¹ *Liber ad Scapulam*, cap. ii, P. L., vol i, col. 699
² *Contra Celsum*, lib. vii, cap. xxvi.
³ Deut. xvii. 12.
⁴ *Ep.* lxii, *ad Pomponium*, n. 4, P. L., vol. iii, col. 371. Cf. *De unitate Ecclesiæ*, n. 17 seq.; *ibid.*, col. 513 seq.

moral principle of the Gospel, felt that the greatest punishment he could inflict was excommunication.

When Lactantius wrote his *Divinæ Institutiones* in 308, he was too greatly impressed by the outrages of the pagan persecutions not to protest most strongly against the use of force in matters of conscience. He writes: "There is no justification for violence and injury, for religion cannot be imposed by force. It is a matter of the will, which must be influenced by words, not by blows. . . . Why then do they rage, and increase, instead of lessening, their folly? Torture and piety have nothing in common; there is no union possible between truth and violence, justice and cruelty.[1] . . . For they (the persecutors) are aware that there is nothing among men more excellent than religion, and that it ought to be defended with all one's might. But as they are deceived in the matter of religion itself, so also are they in the manner of its defence. For religion is to be defended, not by putting to death, but by dying; not by cruelty but by patient endurance; not by crime but by faith. . . . If you wish to defend religion by bloodshed, by tortures and by crime, you no longer defend it, but pollute and profane it. For nothing is so much a matter of free will as religion."[2]

An era of official toleration began a few years later, when Constantine published the Edict of Milan (313), which placed Christianity and Paganism on practically the same footing. But the Emperor did not always observe this law of toleration, whereby he hoped to restore the peace of the Empire. A convert to Chris-

[1] Cf. Pascal, *Lettre provinciale*, xii.
[2] *Divin. Institut.*, lib. v, cap. xx.

tian views and policy, he thought it his duty to interfere in the doctrinal and ecclesiastical quarrels of the day; and he claimed the title and assumed the functions of a Bishop in externals. "You are Bishops," he said one day, addressing a number of them, "whose jurisdiction is within the Church; I also am a Bishop, ordained by God to oversee whatever is external to the Church."[1] This assumption of power frequently worked positive harm to the Church, although Constantine always pretended to further her interests.

When Arianism began to make converts of the Christian emperors, they became very bitter toward the Catholic bishops. We are not at all astonished, therefore, that one of the victims of this new persecution, St. Hilary, of Poitiers, expressly repudiated and condemned this régime of violence. He also proclaimed, in the name of ecclesiastical tradition, the principle of religious toleration. He deplored the fact that men in his day believed that they could defend the rights of God and the Gospel of Jesus Christ by worldly intrigue. He writes: "I ask you Bishops to tell me, whose favor did the Apostles seek in preaching the Gospel, and on whose power did they rely to preach Jesus Christ? To-day, alas! while the power of the State enforces divine faith, men say that Christ is powerless. The Church threatens exile and imprisonment; she in whom men formerly believed while in exile and prison, now wishes to make men believe her by force. . . . She is now exiling the very priests who once spread her gospel. What a striking contrast between the Church of the past and the Church of to-day."[2]

[1] Eusebius, *Vita Constantini*, lib. iv, cap. xxiv.
[2] *Liber contra Auxentium*, cap. iv.

This protest is the outcry of a man who had suffered from the intolerance of the civil power, and who had learned by experience how even a Christian State may hamper the liberty of the Church, and hinder the true progress of the Gospel.

To sum up: As late as the middle of the fourth century and even later, all the Fathers and ecclesiastical writers who discuss the question of toleration are opposed to the use of force. To a man they reject absolutely the death penalty, and enunciate that principle which was to prevail in the Church down the centuries, *i.e.*, *Ecclesia abhorret a sanguine*[1] (the Church has a horror of bloodshed); and they declare faith must be absolutely free, and conscience a domain wherein violence must never enter.[2]

The stern laws of the Old Testament have been abolished by the New.

[1] *Canons of Hippolytus*, in the third or fourth century, no. 74-75; Duchesne, *Les origines du culte chrétien*, 2ᵉ ed., p. 309; Lactantius, *Divin. Institut.*, lib. vi, cap. xx.
[2] Lactantius, *Divin. Institut.*, lib. v, cap. xx.

CHAPTER II

SECOND PERIOD

From Valentinian I to Theodosius II

The Church and the Criminal Code of the Christian Emperors against Heresy

Constantine considered himself a bishop in externals. His Christian successors inherited this title, and acted in accordance with it. One of them, Theodosius II, voiced their mind when he said that " the first duty of the imperial majesty was to protect the true religion, whose worship was intimately connected with the prosperity of human undertakings." [1]

This concept of the State implied the vigorous prosecution of heresy. We therefore see the Christian emperors severely punishing all those who denied the orthodox faith, or rather their own faith, which they considered, rightly or wrongly, the faith of the Church.

From the reign of Valentinian I, and especially from the reign of Theodosius I, the laws against heretics continued to increase with surprising regularity. As many as sixty-eight were enacted in fifty-seven years. They punished every form of heresy, whether it merely differed from the orthodox faith in some minor detail, or whether it resulted in a social up-

---

[1] Theodosii II, *Novellæ*, tit. iii. (438).

heaval. The penalties differed in severity; *i. e.*, exile, confiscation, the inability to transmit property. There were different degrees of exile; from Rome, from the cities, from the Empire. The legislators seemed to think that some sects would die out completely, if they were limited solely to country places. But the severer penalties, like the death penalty, were reserved for those heretics who were disturbers of the public peace, *v. g.*, the Manicheans and the Donatists. The Manicheans, with their dualistic theories, and their condemnation of marriage and its consequences, were regarded as enemies of the State; a law of 428 treated them as criminals " who had reached the highest degree of rascality."

The Donatists, who in Africa had incited the mob of Circumcelliones to destroy the Catholic churches, had thrown that part of the Empire into the utmost disorder. The State could not regard with indifference such an armed revolution. Several laws were passed, putting the Donatists on a par with the Manicheans, and in one instance both were declared guilty of the terrible crime of treason. But the death penalty was chiefly confined to certain sects of the Manicheans. This law did not affect private opinions (except in the case of the Encratites, the Saccophori, and the Hydroparastatæ), but only those who openly practiced this heretical cult. The State did not claim the right of entering the secret recesses of a man's conscience. This law is all the more worthy of remark, inasmuch as Diocletian had legislated more severely against the Manicheans in his Edict of 287: "We thus decree," he writes Julianus, "against these men, whose doctrines and whose magical arts you have made known

THE INQUISITION

to us: the leaders are to be burned with their books, their followers are to be put to death, or sent to the mines." In comparison with such a decree, the legislation of the Christian Emperors was rather moderate.

It is somewhat difficult to ascertain how far these laws were enforced by the various Emperors. Besides, we are only concerned with the spirit which inspired them. The State considered itself the protector of the Church, and in this capacity placed its sword at the service of the orthodox faith. It is our purpose to find out what the churchman of the day thought of this attitude of the State.

The religious troubles caused chiefly by three heresies, Manicheism, Donatism, and Priscillianism, gave them ample opportunity of expressing their opinions.

. . . .

The Manicheans, driven from Rome and Milan, took refuge in Africa. It must be admitted that many of them by their depravity merited the full severity of the law. The initiated, or the *elect*, as they were called, gave themselves up to unspeakable crimes. A number of them on being arrested at Carthage confessed immoral practices that would not bear repetition, and this debauchery was not peculiar to a few wicked followers, but was merely the carrying out of the Manichean ritual, which other heretics likewise admitted.[1]

The Church in Africa was not at all severe in its general treatment of the sect. St. Augustine, especially, never called upon the civil power to suppress it. For

[1] Augustine, *De hæresibus*, Hæres, 46.

he could not forget that he himself had for nine years (373-382), belonged to this sect, whose doctrines and practices he now denounced. He writes the Manicheans: " Let those who have never known the troubles of a mind in search of the truth proceed against you with vigor. It is impossible for me to do so, because for years I was cruelly tossed about by your false doctrines, which I advocated and defended to the best of my ability. I ought to bear with you now, as men bore with me when I blindly accepted your doctrines." [1] All he did was to hold public conferences with their leaders, whose arguments he had no difficulty in refuting.[2]

The conversions obtained in this way were rather numerous, even if all were not equally sincere. All converts from the sect were required, like their successors, the Cathari of the Middle Ages, to denounce their brethren by name, under the threat of being refused the pardon which their formal retraction merited. This denunciation was what we would call to-day " a service for the public good." We, however, know of no case in which the Church made use of this information to punish the one who had been denounced.

.   .   .   .

Donatism (from Donatus, the Bishop of Casæ Nigræ in Numidia) for a time caused more trouble to the Church than Manicheism. It was more of a schism than a heresy. The election to the see of Carthage of the deacon Cæcilian, who was accused of having handed over the Scriptures to the Roman officials

[1] *Contra epistolam Manichæi quam vocant Fundamenti*, n. 2, 3.

[2] Cf. Dom Leclerc, *L'Afrique Chrétienne*, Paris, 1904, vol. ii, pp. 113-122.

during the persecution of Diocletian, was the occasion of the schism. Donatus and his followers wished this nomination annulled, while their opponents defended its validity. Accordingly, two councils were held to decide the question, one at Rome (313), the other at Arles (314). Both decided against the Donatists; they at once appealed to the Emperor, who confirmed the decrees of the two councils (316). The schismatics in their anger rose in rebellion, and a number of them known as Circumcelliones went about stirring the people to revolt. But neither Constantine nor his successors were inclined to allow armed rebellion to go unchallenged. The Donatists were punished to the full extent of the law. They had been the first, remarks St. Augustine, to invoke the aid of the secular arm. "They met with the same fate as the accusers of Daniel; the lions turned against them."[1]

We need not linger over the details of this conflict, in which crimes were committed on both sides. The Donatists, bitterly prosecuted by the State, declared its action cruel and unjust. St. Optatus thus answers them: "Will you tell me that it is not lawful to defend the rights of God by the death penalty? . . . If killing is an evil, the guilty ones are themselves the cause of it."[2] "It is impossible," you say, "for the State to inflict the death penalty in the name of God," —But was it not in God's name that Moses,[3] Phinees,[4] and Elias[5] put to death the worshipers of the golden

[1] *Ep.* clxxxv, n. 7.
[2] *De Schismate Donatistarum*, lib. iii, cap. vi.
[3] Exod. xxxii. 28.
[4] Numb. xxv. 7–9.
[5] 3 Kings xviii. 40.

calf, and the apostates of the Old Law?—"These times are altogether different," you reply; "the New Law must not be confounded with the Old. Did not Christ forbid St. Peter to use the sword?"[1] Yes, undoubtedly, but Christ came to suffer, not to defend Himself.[2] The lot of Christians is different from that of Christ.

It is in virtue, therefore, of the Old Law that St. Optatus defends the State's interference in religious questions, and its infliction of the death penalty upon heretics. This is evidently a different teaching from the doctrine of toleration held by the Fathers of the preceding age. But the other bishops of Africa did not share his views.

In his dealings with the Donatists, St. Augustine was at first absolutely tolerant, as he had been with the Manicheans. He thought he could rely upon their good faith, and conquer their prejudices by an honest discussion. "We have no intention," he writes to a Donatist bishop, "of forcing men to enter our communion against their will. I am desirous that the State cease its bitter persecution, but you in turn ought to cease terrorizing us by your band of Circumcelliones. . . . Let us discuss our differences from the standpoint of reason and the sacred Scriptures."[3]

In one of his works, now lost, *Contra partem Donati*, he maintains that it is wrong for the State to force schismatics to come back to the Church.[4] At the most, he was ready to admit the justice of the law of Theodosius, which imposed a fine of ten gold pieces upon those schismatics who had committed open acts of

[1] John xviii. 11.
[2] *De Schismate Don.*, cap. vii.
[3] *Ep.* xxiii, n. 7.
[4] Retract. lib. II, cap. v.

THE INQUISITION

violence. But no man was to be punished by the State for private heretical opinions.[1]

The imperial laws were carried out in some cities of North Africa, because many of St. Augustine's colleagues did not share his views. Many Donatists were brought back to the fold by these vigorous measures. St. Augustine, seeing that in some cases the use of force proved more beneficial than his policy of absolute toleration, changed his views, and formulated his theory of moderate persecution: *temperata severitas*.[2]

Heretics and schismatics, he maintained, were to be regarded as sheep who had gone astray. It is the shepherd's duty to run after them, and bring them back to the fold by using, if occasion require it, the whip and the goad.[3] There is no need of using cruel tortures like the rack, the iron pincers, or sending them to the stake; flogging is sufficient. Besides this mode of punishment is not at all cruel, for it is used by schoolmasters, parents, and even by bishops while presiding as judges in their tribunals.[4]

In his opinion, the severest penalty that ought to be inflicted upon the Donatists is exile for their bishops and priests, and fines for their followers. He strongly denounced the death penalty as contrary to Christian charity.[5]

Both the imperial officers and the Donatists themselves objected to this theory.

The officers of the Emperor wished to apply the law in all its rigor, and to sentence the schismatics to

[1] *Ep.* clxxxv, n. 25.
[2] *Ep.* xciii, n. 10.
[3] *Ep.* clxxxv, n. 23.
[4] *Ep.* cxxxiii, n. 2.
[5] *Ep.* clxxxv, n. 26; *Ep.* xciii, n. 10.

death, when they deemed it proper. St. Augustine adjures them, in the name of "Christian and Catholic meekness"[1] not to go to this extreme, no matter how great the crimes of the Donatists had been. "You have penalties enough," he writes, "exile, for instance, without torturing their bodies or putting them to death."[2]

And when the proconsul Apringius quoted St. Paul to justify the use of the sword, St. Augustine replied: "The apostle has well said, 'for he beareth not the sword in vain.'[3] But we must carefully distinguish between temporal and spiritual affairs."[4] "Because it is just to inflict the death penalty for crimes against the common law, it does not follow that it is right to put heretics and schismatics to death." "Punish the guilty ones, but do not put them to death." "For," he writes another proconsul, "if you decide upon putting them to death, you will thereby prevent our denouncing them before your tribunal. They will then rise up against us with greater boldness. And if you tell us that we must either denounce them or risk death at their hands, we will not hesitate a moment, but will choose death ourselves."[5]

Despite these impassioned appeals for mercy, some Donatists were put to death. This prompted the schismatics everywhere to deny that the State had any right to inflict the death penalty or any other penalty upon them.[6]

[1] *Ep.* clxxxv, n. 26; *Ep.* cxxxix, n. 2.
[2] *Ep.* cxxxiii, n. 1.
[3] Rom. xiii. 4.
[4] *Ep.* cxxxiv, n. 3.
[5] *Ep.* c, n. 2; cf. *Ep.* cxxxix, n. 2.
[6] *Contra Epistolam Parmeniani*, lib. i, cap. xvi.

THE INQUISITION

St. Augustine at once undertook to defend the rights of the State. He declared that the death penalty, which on principle he disapproved, might in some instances be lawfully inflicted. Did not the crimes of some of these rebellious schismatics merit the most extreme penalty of the law? " They kill the souls of men, and the State merely tortures their bodies; they cause eternal death, and then complain when the State makes them suffer temporal death." [1]

But this is only an argument *ad hominem*. St. Augustine means to say that, even if the Donatists were put to death, they had no reason to complain. He does not admit, in fact, that they had been cruelly treated. The victims they allege are false martyrs or suicides.[2] He denounces those Catholics who, outside of cases of self-defense, had murdered their opponents.[3]

The State also has the perfect right to impose the lesser penalties of flogging, fines, and exile. " For he (the prince) beareth not the sword in vain," says the Apostle. " For he is God's minister; an avenger to execute wrath upon him that doeth evil." [4] It is not true to claim that St: Paul here meant merely the spiritual sword of excommunication.[5] The context proves clearly that he was speaking of the material sword. Schism and heresy are crimes which, like poisoning, are punishable by the State.[6] Princes must render an account to God for the way they govern.

[1] *In Joann. Tractat.* xi, cap. xv.
[2] *Ibid.*
[3] *Ep.* lxxxvii, n. 8.
[4] Rom. xiii; 4. Augustine, *Contra litteras Petiliani*, lib. ii, cap. lxxxiii–lxxxiv; *Contra Epist. Parmeniani*, lib. i, cap. xvi.
[5] *Contra Epist. Parmeniani, ibid.*
[6] *Ibid.*

It is natural that they should desire the peace of the Church, their mother, who gave them spiritual life.[1]

The State, therefore, has the right to suppress heresy, because the public tranquillity is disturbed by religious dissensions.[2] Her intervention also works for the good of individuals. For, on the one hand, there are some sincere but timid souls who are prevented by their environment from abandoning their schism; they are encouraged to return to the fold by the civil power, which frees them from a most humiliating bondage.[3]

On the other hand, there are many schismatics in good faith who would never attain the truth unless they were forced to enter into themselves and examine their false position. The civil power admonishes such souls to abandon their errors; it does not punish them for any crime.[4] The Church's rebellious children are not forced to believe, but are induced by a salutary fear to listen to the true doctrine.[5]

Conversions obtained in this way are none the less sincere. Undoubtedly, absolute toleration is best in theory, but in practice a certain amount of coercion is more helpful to souls. We must judge both methods by their fruits.

In a word, St. Augustine was at first, by temperament, an advocate of absolute toleration, but later on experience led him to prefer a mitigated form of coercion. When his opponents objected—using words

[1] *In Joann. Tractatus* xi, cap. xiv.
[2] *Ep.* lxxxii, n. 8.
[3] *Ep.* clxxxv, n. 13.
[4] *Ep.* xciii, n. 10.
[5] *Contra litteras Petiliani*, lib. ii, cap. lxxxiii; *Ep.* clxxxv, n. 21; *Ep.* xciii, n. 4.

similar to those of St. Hilary and the early Fathers
—that "the true Church suffered persecution, but did
not persecute," [1] he quoted Sara's persecution of Agar.[2]
He was wrong to quote the Old Testament as his
authority. But we ought at least be thankful that he
did not cite other instances more incompatible with
the charity of the Gospel. His instinctive Christian
horror of the death penalty kept him from making
this mistake.

. . . .

Priscillianism brought out clearly the views current
in the fourth century regarding the punishment due
to heresy. Very little was known of Priscillian until
lately; and despite the publication of several of his
works in 1889, he still remains an enigmatical personality.[3] His erudition and critical spirit were, however, so remarkable, that an historian of weight declares that henceforth we must rank him with St.
Jerome.[4] But his writings were, in all probability, far
from orthodox. We can easily find in them traces of
Gnosticism and Manicheism. He was accused of
Manicheism although he anathematized Manes. He
was likewise accused of magic. He denied the charge,
and declared that every magician deserved death,
according to Exodus: "Wizards thou shalt not suffer
to live."[5] He little dreamt when he wrote these words
that he was pronouncing his own death sentence.

[1] *Ep.* clxxxv, n. 10.
[2] *Ibid.*, n. 11.
[3] On Priscillian and his work, cf. Dom Leclerc, *L'Espagne Chrétienne*, Paris, 1906, ch. iii; Friedrich Paret, *Priscillianus*, Würzburg, 1891; Kuenstle, *Antipriscilliana*, Freiburg, 1905.
[4] Cf. Leclerc, p. 164.
[5] Exod. xxii. 18.

Although condemned by the council of Saragossa (380), he nevertheless became bishop of Abila. Later on, he went to Rome to plead his cause before Pope Damasus, but was refused a hearing. He next turned to St. Ambrose, who likewise would not hearken to his defense.[1] In 385 a council was assembled at Bordeaux to consider his case anew. He at once appealed to the Emperor, "so as not to be judged by the bishops," as Sulpicius Severus tells us, a fatal mistake which cost him his life.

He was then conducted to the Emperor at Treves, where he was tried before a secular court, bishops Idacius and Ithacius appearing as his accusers. St. Martin, who was in Treves at the time, was scandalized that a purely ecclesiastical matter should be tried before a secular judge. His biographer, Sulpicius Severus, tells us "that he kept urging Ithacius to withdraw his accusation." He also entreated Maximus not to shed the blood of these unfortunates, for the bishops could meet the difficulty by driving the heretics from the churches. He asserted that to make the State judge in a matter of doctrine was a cruel, unheard-of violation of the divine law.

As long as St. Martin remained in Treves, the trial was put off, and before he left the city, he made Maximus promise not to shed the blood of Priscillian and his companions. But soon after St. Martin's departure, the Emperor, instigated by the relentless bishops Rufus and Magnus, forgot his promise of mercy, and entrusted the case to the prefect Evodius, a cruel and hard-hearted official. Priscillian appeared before him

[1] Cf. Sulp. Sev. *Chronicon*, ii, P. L., vol. xx, col. 155–159; *Dialogi*, iii, 11–23, *ibid.*, col. 217–219.

twice, *and was convicted of the crime of magic.* He was made to confess under torture that he had given himself up to magical arts, and that he had prayed naked before women in midnight assemblies. Evodius declared him guilty, and placed him under guard until the evidence had been presented to the Emperor. After reading the records of the trial, Maximus declared that Priscillian and his companions deserved death. Ithacius, perceiving how unpopular he would make himself with his fellow-bishops, if he continued to play the part of prosecutor in a capital case, withdrew. A new trial was therefore ordered. This subterfuge of the Bishop did not change matters at all, because by this time the case had been practically settled. Patricius, the imperial treasurer, presided at the second trial. On his findings, Priscillian and some of his followers were condemned to death. Others of the sect were exiled.

This deplorable trial is often brought forward as an argument against the Church. It is important, therefore, for us to ascertain its precise character, and to discover who was to blame for it.

The real cause of Priscillian's condemnation was the accusation of heresy made by a Catholic bishop. Technically, he was tried in the secular courts for the crime of magic, but the State could not condemn him to death on any other charge, once Ithacius had ceased to appear against him.

It is right, therefore, to attribute Priscillian's death to the action of an individual bishop, but it is altogether unjust to hold the Church responsible.[1]

[1] Bernays, *Ueber die Chronik des Sulp. Sev.*, Berlin, 1861, p. 13, was the first to point out that Priscillian was condemned not

20   THE INQUISITION

In this way contemporary writers viewed the matter. The Christians of the fourth century were all but unanimous, says an historian,[1] in denouncing the penalty inflicted in this famous trial. Sulpicius Severus, despite his horror of the Priscillianists, repeats over and over again that their condemnation was a deplorable example; he even stigmatizes it as a crime. St. Ambrose speaks just as strongly.[2] We know how vehemently St. Martin disapproved of the attitude of Ithacius and the Emperor Maximus; he refused for a long time to hold communion with the bishops who had in any way taken part in the condemnation of Priscillian.[3] Even in Spain, where public opinion was so divided, Ithacius was everywhere denounced. At first some defended him on the plea of the public good, and on account of the high authority of those who judged the case. But after a time he became so generally hated that, despite his excuse that he merely followed the advice of others, he was driven from his bishopric.[4] This outburst of popular indignation proves conclusively that, if the Church did call upon the aid of the secular arm in religious questions, she did not authorize it to use the sword against heretics.

The blood of Priscillian was the seed of Priscillianism. But his disciples certainly went further than their master; they became thoroughgoing Manicheans This explains St. Jerome's[5] and St. Augustine's[6] strong

for heresy, but for the crime of magic. This is the commonly received view to-day.

[1] Puéch, *Journal des Savants*, May 1891, p. 250.
[2] Cf. Gams, *Kirchengeschichte von Spanien*, vol. ii, p. 382.
[3] Sulpicius Severus, *Dialogi* iii, 11–13.
[4] Sulp. Sev., *Chronicon*, loc. cit.
[5] *De Viris illustribus*, 121–123.
[6] *De hæresibus*, cap. 70.

denunciations of the Spanish heresy. The gross errors of the Priscillianists in the fifth century attracted in 447 the attention of Pope St. Leo. He reproaches them for breaking the bonds of marriage, rejecting all idea of chastity, and contravening all rights, human and divine. He evidently held Priscillian responsible for all these teachings. That is why he rejoices in the fact that " the secular princes, horrified at this sacrilegious folly, executed the author of these errors with several of his followers." He even declares that this action of the State is helpful to the Church. He writes: "The Church, in the spirit of Christ, ought to denounce heretics, but should never put them to death; still the severe laws of Christian princes redound to her good, for some heretics, through fear of punishment, are won back to the true faith."[1] St. Leo in this passage is rather severe. While he does not yet require the death penalty for heresy, he accepts it in the name of the public good. It is greatly to be feared that the churchmen of the future will go a great deal further.

The Church is endeavoring to state her position accurately on the suppression of heresy. She declares that nothing will justify her shedding of human blood. This is evident from the conduct and writings of St. Augustine, St. Martin, St. Ambrose, St. Leo (*cruentas refugit ultiones*), and Ithacius himself. But to what extent should she accept the aid of the civil power, when it undertakes to defend her teachings by force?

Some writers, like St. Optatus of Mileve, and Priscillian, later on the victim of his own teaching, believed that the Christian State ought to use the sword against

[1] *Ep.* xv, *ad Turribium*, P. L., vol. liv, col. 679-680.

heretics guilty of crimes against the public welfare; and, strangely enough, they quote the Old Testament as their authority. Without giving his approval to this theory, St. Leo the Great did not condemn the practical application of it in the case of the Priscillianists. The Church, according to him, while assuming no responsibility for them, reaped the benefit of the rigorous measures taken by the State.

But most of the Bishops absolutely condemned the infliction of the death penalty for heresy, even if the heresy was incidentally the cause of social disturbances. Such was the view of St. Augustine,[1] St. Martin, St. Ambrose, many Spanish bishops, and a bishop of Gaul named Theognitus;[2] in a word, of all who disapproved of the condemnation of Priscillian. As a rule, they protested in the name of Christian charity; they voiced the new spirit of the Gospel of Christ. At the other extremity of the Catholic world, St. John Chrysostom re-echoes their teaching. "To put a heretic to death," he says, "is an unpardonable crime."[3]

But in view of the advantage to the Church, either from the maintenance of the public peace, or from the conversion of individuals, the State may employ a certain amount of force against heretics.

"God forbids us to put them to death," continues St. Chrysostom, "just as he forbade the servants to gather up the cockle,"[4] because he regards their conversion as possible; but he does not forbid us doing all in our power to prevent their public meetings, and

---

[1] *Ep.* c, n. 1.
[2] Cf. Sulpicius Severus, *Dialogi*, iii, 12, *loc. cit.*, col. 218.
[3] *Homilia* xlvi, *in Matthæum*, cap. i.
[4] *Ibid.*, cap. ii.

their preaching of false doctrine. St. Augustine adds that they may be punished by fine and exile.

To this extent the churchmen of the day accepted the aid of the secular arm. Nor were they content with merely accepting it. They declared that the State had not only the right to help the Church in suppressing heresy, but that she was in duty bound to do so. In the seventh century, St. Isidore of Seville discusses this question in practically the same terms as St. Augustine.[1]

---

[1] We think it important to give Lea's résumé of this period. It will show how a writer, although trying to be impartial, may distort the facts: "It was only sixty-two years after the slaughter of Priscillian and his followers had excited so much horror, that Leo I, when the heresy seemed to be reviving, in 447, not only justified the act, but declared that *if the followers of heresy so damnable were allowed to live*, there would be an end to human and divine law. The final step had been taken, and *the Church was definitely pledged to the suppression of heresy at whatever cost*. It is impossible not to attribute to ecclesiastical influence the successive Edicts by which, from the time of Theodosius the Great, persistence in heresy was punished by death. A powerful impulse to this development is to be found in the responsibility which grew upon the Church from its connection with the State. When it could influence the monarch and procure from him Edicts condemning heretics to exile, to the mines, *and even to death*, it felt that God had put into its hands powers to be exercised and not to be neglected" (vol. i, p. 215). If we read carefully the words of St. Leo (p. 27, note 1), we shall see that the Emperors are responsible for the words that Lea ascribes to the Pope. It is hard to understand how he can assert that the imperial Edicts decreeing the death penalty are due to ecclesiastical influence, when we notice that nearly all the churchmen of the day protested against such a penalty

CHAPTER III

THIRD PERIOD

From 1100 to 1250

The Revival of the Manichean Heresies in the Middle Ages

From the sixth to the eleventh century, heretics, with the exception of certain Manichean sects, were hardly ever persecuted.[1] In the sixth century, for instance, the Arians lived side by side with the Catholics, under the protection of the State, in a great many Italian cities, especially in Ravenna and Pavia.[2]

During the Carlovingian period, we come across a few heretics, but they gave little trouble.

The *Adoptianism* of Elipandus, Archbishop of Toledo, and Felix, Bishop of Urgel, was abandoned by its authors, after it had been condemned by Pope Adrian I, and several provincial councils.[3]

A more important heresy arose in the ninth century. Godescalcus, a monk of Orbais, in the diocese of

[1] In 556, Manicheans were put to death at Ravenna, in accordance with the laws of Justinian.

[2] We may still visit at Ravenna the Arian and Catholic baptisteries of the sixth century. Cf. Gregorii Magni *Dialogi*, iii, cap. xxix, *Mon. Germ., ibid.*, pp. 534–535.

[3] Einhard: *Annales*, ann. 792, in the *Mon. Germ. SS.*, vol. i, p. 179.

Soissons, taught that Jesus Christ did not die for all men. His errors on predestination were condemned as heretical by the Council of Mainz (848); and Quierzy (849); and he himself was sentenced to be flogged and then imprisoned for life in the monastery of Hautvilliers.[1] But this punishment of flogging was a purely ecclesiastical penalty. Archbishop Hincmar, in ordering it, declared that he was acting in accordance with the rule of St. Benedict, and a canon of the Council of Agde.

The imprisonment to which Godescalcus was subjected was likewise a monastic punishment. Practically, it did not imply much more than the confinement strictly required by the rules of his convent. It is interesting to note that imprisonment for crime is of purely ecclesiastical origin. The Roman law knew nothing of it. It was at first a penalty peculiar to monks and clerics, although later on laymen also were subjected to it.

About the year 1000, the Manicheans, under various names, came from Bulgaria, and spread over western Europe.[2] We meet them about this time in Italy, Spain, France, and Germany. Public sentiment soon became bitter against them, and they became the victims of a general, though intermittent, persecution. Orléans, Arras, Cambrai, Châlons, Goslai, Liège, Soissons, Ravenna, Monteforte, Asti, and Toulouse became the field of their propaganda, and often the place of their execution. Several heretics like Peter

[1] " In nostra parochia . . . monasteriali costudiæ mancipatus est." Hincmar's letter to Pope Nicholas I, *Hincmari Opera*, ed. Sirmond, Paris, 1645, vol. ii, p. 262.

[2] Cf. C. Schmidt, *Histoire et doctrine de la secte des Cathares*, vol. i, pp. 16–54, 82.

of Bruys, Henry of Lausanne, Arnold of Brescia, and Éon de l'Étoile (Eudo de Stella), likewise troubled the Church, who to stop their bold propaganda used force herself, or permitted the State or the people to use it.

It was at Orléans in 1022 that Catholics for the first time during this period treated heretics with cruelty. An historian of the time assures us that this cruelty was due to both king and people: *regis jussu et universæ plebis consensu.*[1] King Robert, dreading the disastrous effects of heresy upon his kingdom, and the consequent loss of souls, sent thirteen of the principal clerics and laymen of the town to the stake. It has been pointed out that this penalty was something unheard-of at the time. " Robert was therefore the originator of the punishment which he decreed."[2] It might be said, however, that this penalty originated with the people, and that the king merely followed out the popular will.

For, as an old chronicler tells us, this execution at Orléans, was not an isolated fact; in other places the populace hunted out heretics, and burned them outside the city walls.[3]

Several years later, the heretics who swarmed into the diocese of Châlons attracted the attention of the Bishop of the city, who was puzzled how to deal with them. He consulted Wazo, the Bishop of Liège, who

---

[1] Raoul Glaber, *Hist.*, lib. iii, cap. viii, *Hist. des Gaules*, vol. x, p. 38. For other authorities consult Julien Havet, *L'hérésie et le bras séculier au moyen âge*, in his *Œuvres*, Paris, 1896, vol. ii, pp. 128-130.

[2] Julien Havet, *op. cit.*, pp. 128, 129.

[3] *Cartulaire de l'abbaye de Saint-Père de Chartres*, ed. Guérard, vol. i, p. 108 and seq.; cf. *Hist. des Gaules*, vol. x, p. 539.

THE INQUISITION

tells us that the French were "infuriated" against heretics. These words would seem to prove that the heretics of the day were prosecuted more vigorously than the documents we possess go to show. It is probable that the Bishop of Châlons detested the "fury" of the persecutors. We will see later on the answer that Wazo sent him.

During the Christmas holidays of 1051 and 1052, a number of Manicheans or Cathari, as they were called, were executed at Goslar, after they had refused to renounce their errors. Instead of being burned, as in France, "they were hanged."

These heretics were executed by the orders of Henry III, and in his presence. But the chronicler of the event remarks that every one applauded the Emperor's action, because he had prevented the spread of the leprosy of heresy, and thus saved many souls.[1]

Twenty-five years later, in 1076 or 1077, a Catharan of the district of Cambrai appeared before the Bishop of Cambrai and his clerics, and was condemned as a heretic. The Bishop's officers and the crowd at once seized him, led him outside the city's gates, and while he knelt and calmly prayed, they burned him at the stake.[2]

A little while before this the Archbishop of Ravenna accused a man named Vilgard of heresy, but what the result of the trial was, we cannot discover. But we do know that during this period other persons were

[1] HERIMAN, Aug. *Chronicon*, ann. 1052, *Mon. Germ. SS.*, vol. v, p. 130. Cf. LAMBERTI, *Annales*, 1053, *ibid.*, p. 155.

[2] Chronicon S. Andreæ Camerac., iii, 3, in the *Mon. Germ. SS.*, vol. vii, p. 540.

We have a letter of Gregory VII in which he denounces the irregular character of this execution. *Ibid.*, p. 540, n. 31.

prosecuted for heresy, and that they were beheaded or sent to the stake.

At Monteforte near Asti, the Cathari had, about 1034, an important settlement. The Marquis Mainfroi, his brother, the Bishop of Asti, and several noblemen of the city, united to attack the castrum; they captured a number of heretics, and on their refusing to return to the orthodox faith, they sent them to the stake.

Other followers of the sect were arrested by the officers of Eriberto, the Archbishop of Milan, who endeavored to win them back to the Catholic faith. Instead of being converted, they tried to spread their heresy throughout the city. The civil magistrates, realizing their corrupting influence, had a stake erected in the public square with a cross in front of it; and in spite of the Archbishop's protest, they required the heretics either to reverence the cross they had blasphemed, or to enter the flaming pile. Some were converted, but the majority of them, covering their faces with their hands, threw themselves into the flames, and were soon burned to ashes.

Few details have come down to us concerning the fate of the Manicheans arrested at this time in Sardinia and in Spain; *exterminati sunt*, says a chronicler.[1]

The Cathari of Toulouse were also arrested, and executed. A few years later, in 1114, the Bishop of Soissons arrested a number of heretics and cast them into prison until he could make up his mind how to

---

[1] "Exterminati sunt," says Raoul Glaber, *Hist.*, lib. ii, cap. xii, *Hist. des Gaules*, vol. x, p. 23.

Exterminati may mean *banished* as well as *put to death*. The context, however, seems to refer to the death penalty.

deal with them. While he was absent at Beauvais, asking the advice of his fellow-bishops assembled there in council, the populace, fearing the weakness of the clergy, attacked the prison, dragged forth the heretics, and burned them at the stake. Guibert de Nogent does not blame them in the least. He simply calls attention to "the just zeal" shown on this occasion by "the people of God," to stop the spread of heresy.

In 1144 the Bishop of Liège, Adalbero II, compelled a number of Cathari to confess their heresy; "he hoped," he said, "with the grace of God, to lead them to repent." But the populace, less kindly-hearted, rushed upon them, and proceeded to burn them at the stake; the Bishop had the greatest difficulty to save the majority of them. He then wrote to Pope Lucius II asking him what was the proper penalty for heresy.[1] We do not know what answer he received.

About the same time a similar dispute arose between the Archbishop and the people of Cologne regarding two or three heretics who had been arrested and condemned. The clergy asked them to return to the Church. But the people, "moved by an excess of zeal," says an historian of the time, seized them, and despite the Archbishop and his clerics led them to the stake. "And marvelous to relate," continues the chronicler, "they suffered their tortures at the stake, not only with patience, but with joy."[2]

One of the most famous heretics of the twelfth century was Peter of Bruys. His hostility toward

[1] Letter of the church of Liège to Pope Lucius II, in MARTÈNE, *Amplissima collectio*, vol. i, col. 776-777.
[2] Letter of Evervin, provost of Steinfeld to St. Bernard, cap. ii, in *Bernardi Opera*, MIGNE, P. L., vol. clxxxii, col. 677.

the clergy helped his propaganda in Gascony. To show his contempt for the Catholic religion, he burned a great number of crosses one Good Friday, and roasted meat in the flames. This angered the people against him. He was seized and burned at St. Giles about the year 1126.[1]

Henry of Lausanne was his most illustrious disciple. We have told the story of his life elsewhere.[2] St. Bernard opposed him vigorously, and succeeded in driving him from the chief cities of Toulouse and the Albigeois, where he carried on his harmful propaganda. He was arrested a short time afterwards (1145 or 1146), and sentenced to life imprisonment, either in one of the prisons of the Archbishop, or in some monastery of Toulouse.

Arnold of Brescia busied himself more with questions of discipline than with dogma; the only reforms he advocated were social reforms.[3] He taught that the clergy should not hold temporal possessions, and he endeavored to drive the papacy from Rome. In this conflict, which involved the property of ecclesiastics and the temporal power of the Church, he was, although successful for a time, finally vanquished.[4] St. Bernard invoked the aid of the secular arm to rid France of him. Later on Pope Eugenius III excommunicated him. He was executed during the pontificate of Adrian IV, in 1155. He was arrested in the city of Rome

[1] Peter the Venerable, Letter to the Archbishops of Arles and Embrum, etc., in the *Hist. des Gaules*, vol. xv, p. 640.

[2] *Vie de Saint Bernard*, 1st edit., Paris, 1895, vol. ii, pp. 218-233.

[3] For details concerning Arnold of Brescia, cf. Vacandard, *Vie de Saint Bernard*, vol. ii, pp. 235-258, 465-469.

[4] Otto Frising, *Gesta Friderici*, lib. ii, cap. xx. Cf. *Historia Pontificalis*, in the *Mon. Germ. SS.*, vol. xx, p. 538

after a riot which was quelled by the Emperor Frederic, now the ally of the Pope, and condemned to be strangled by the prefect of the city. His body was then burned, and his ashes thrown into the Tiber, "for fear," says a writer of the time, "the people would gather them up, and honor them as the ashes of a martyr." [1]

In 1148, the Council of Rheims judged the case of the famous Éon de l'Etoile (Eudo de Stella). This strange individual had acquired a reputation for sanctity while living a hermit's life. One day, struck by the words of the liturgy, *Per Eum qui venturus est judicare vivos et mortuos*, he conceived the idea that he was the Son of God. He made some converts among the lowest classes, who, not content with denying the faith, soon began to pillage the churches. Éon was arrested for causing these disturbances, and was brought before Pope Eugenius III, then presiding over the Council of Rheims. He was judged insane, and in all kindness was placed under the charge of Suger, the Abbot of St. Denis. He was confined to a monastery, where he died soon after.

Strangely enough, some of his disciples persisted in believing in him; "they preferred to die rather than renounce their belief," says an historian of the time. They were handed over to the secular arm and perished at the stake. In decreeing this penalty, the civil power was undoubtedly influenced by the example of Robert the Pious.

It is easy to determine the responsibility of the Church, *i. e.*, her bishops and priests, in this series of

[1] Boso, *Vita Hadriani*, in Watterich, *Romanorum pontificum Vitæ*, vol. ii, pp. 326, 330.

executions (1020 to 1150). At Orléans, the populace and the king put the heretics to death; the historians of the time tell us plainly that the clergy merely declared the orthodox doctrine. It was the same at Goslar. At Asti, the Bishop's name appears with the names of the other nobles who had the Cathari executed, but it seems certain that he exercised no special authority in the case. At Milan, the civil magistrates themselves, against the Archbishop's protest, gave the heretics the choice between reverencing the cross, and the stake.

At Soissons, the populace, feeling certain that the clergy would not resort to extreme measures, profited by the Bishop's absence to burn the heretics they detested. At Liège, the Bishop managed to save a few heretics from the violence of the angry mob. At Cologne, the Archbishop was not so successful; the people rose in their anger and burned the heretics before they could be tried. Peter of Bruys and the Manichean at Cambrai were both put to death by the people. Arnold of Brescia, deserted by fortune, fell a victim to his political adversaries; the prefect of Rome was responsible for his execution.[1]

[1] The case of Arnold, however, is not so clear. The *Annales Augustani minores* (*Mon. Germ. SS.*, vol. x, p. 8) declare that the Pope hanged the rebel. Another anonymous writer (cf. Tanon, *Hist. des tribunaux de l'Inq. en France*, p. 456, n. 2) says with more probability, that Adrian merely degraded him. According to Otto of Freisingen (*Mon. Germ. SS.*, vol. xx, p. 404), Arnold *principis examini reservatus est, ad ultimum a præfecto Urbis ligno adactus*. Finally, Geroch de Reichersberg tells us (*De investigatione Antichristi*, lib. i, cap. xlii, ed. Scheibelberger, 1875, pp. 88–89) that Arnold was taken from the ecclesiastical prison and put to death by the servants of the Roman prefect. In any case, politics rather than religion was the cause of his death.

THE INQUISITION 33

In a word, in all these executions, the Church either kept aloof, or plainly manifested her disapproval.

During this period, we know of only one bishop, Théodwin of Liège, who called upon the secular arm to punish heretics. This is all the more remarkable because his predecessor, Wazo, and his successor, Adalbero II, both protested in word and deed against the cruelty of both sovereign and people.

Wazo, his biographer tells us, strongly condemned the execution of heretics at Goslar, and, had he been there, would have acted as St. Martin of Tours in the case of Priscillian.[1] His reply to the letter of the Bishop of Châlons reveals his inmost thoughts on the subject. "To use the sword of the civil authority," he says, "against the Manicheans,[2] is contrary to the spirit of the Church, and the teaching of her Divine Founder. The Saviour ordered us to let the cockle grow with the good grain until the harvest time, lest in uprooting the cockle we uproot also the wheat with it.[3] Moreover, continues Wazo, those who are cockle to-day may be converted to-morrow, and be garnered in as wheat at the harvest time. Therefore, they should be allowed to live. The only penalty we should use against them is excommunication."[4]

The Bishop of Liège, quoting this parable of Christ which St. Chrysostom had quoted before him, interprets it in a more liberal fashion than the Bishop of Constantinople. For he not only condemns the death penalty, but all recourse to the secular arm.

[1] *Vita Vasonis*, cap. xxv, xxvi, Migne, P. L., vol. cxlii, col. 753.
[2] *Ibid.*, col. 752.
[3] Matt. xiii. 29–30.
[4] *Vita Vasonis, loc. cit.*, col. 753.

Peter Cantor, one of the best minds of northern France in the twelfth century, also protested against the infliction of the death penalty for heresy, "Whether," he says, "the Cathari are proved guilty of heresy, or whether they freely admit their guilt, they ought not to be put to death, unless they attack the Church in armed rebellion." For the Apostle said: "A man that is a heretic, after the first and second admonition, avoid;" he did not say: "Kill him." "Imprison heretics if you will, but do not put them to death." [1]

Geroch of Reichersberg, a famous German of the same period, a disciple and friend of St. Bernard, speaks in a similar strain of the execution of Arnold of Brescia. He was most anxious that the Church, and especially the Roman curia, should not be held responsible for his death. "The priesthood," he says, "ought to refrain from the shedding of blood." There is no doubt whatever that this heretic taught a wicked doctrine, but banishment, imprisonment, or some similar penalty would have been ample punishment for his wrong-doing, without sentencing him to death.

St. Bernard had also asked that Arnold be banished. The execution of heretics at Cologne gave him a chance to state his views on the suppression of heresy. The courage with which these fanatics met death rather disconcerted Evervin, the provost of Steinfeld, who wrote the Abbot of Clairvaux for an explanation.[2]

---

[1] *Verbum abbreviatum*, cap. lxxviii, Migne, P. L., vol. ccv, col. 231.
[2] Evervin's letter in Migne, P. L., vol. clxxxii, col. 676 and seq.

THE INQUISITION

" Their courage," he replies, " arose from mere stubbornness; the devil inspired them with this constancy you speak of, just as he prompted Judas to hang himself. These heretics are not real but counterfeit martyrs (*perfidiæ martyres*). But while I may approve the zeal of the people for the faith, I cannot at all approve their excessive cruelty; for faith is a matter of persuasion, not of force: *fides suadenda est, non imponenda*." [1]

On principle, the Abbot of Clairvaux blames the bishops and even the secular princes, who through indifference or less worthy reasons fail to hunt for the foxes who are ravaging the vineyards of the Savior. But once the guilty ones have been discovered, he declares that only kindness should be used to win them back. " Let us capture them by arguments and not by force," [2] *i. e.*, let us first refute their errors, and if possible bring them back into the fold of the Catholic Church.

If they stubbornly refuse to be converted, let the bishop excommunicate them, to prevent their doing further injury; if occasion require it, let the civil power arrest them and put them in prison. Imprisonment is a severe enough penalty, because it prevents their dangerous propaganda:[3] *aut corrigendi sunt, ne pereant; aut, ne perimant, coercendi.*[4] St. Bernard was always faithful to his own teaching, as we learn from his mission in Languedoc.[5]

---

[1] *In Cantica*, Sermo lxiv, n. 12.

[2] *Ibid.*, n. 8.

[3] *De Consideratione*, lib. iii, cap. i, n. 3.

[4] *Ibid.*; cf. *Ep.* 241 and 242. For more details, cf. Vacandard, *Vie de Saint Bernard*, vol. ii, pp. 211–216, 461–462.

[5] Cf. Vacandard, *op. cit.*, vol. ii, pp. 217–234.

Having ascertained the views of individual churchmen, we now turn to the councils of the period, and find them voicing the self-same teaching. In 1049, the Council held at Rheims by Pope Leo IX declared all heretics excommunicated, but said nothing of any temporal penalty, nor did it empower the secular princes to aid in the suppression of heresy.[1]

The Council of Toulouse in 1119, presided over by Calixtus II, and the General Council of the Lateran, in 1139, were a little more severe; they not only issued a solemn bull of excommunication against heretics, but ordered the civil power to prosecute them: *per potestates exteras coerceri præcipimus*.[2] This order was, undoubtedly an answer to St. Bernard's request of Louis VII to banish Arnold from his kingdom. The only penalty referred to by both these councils was imprisonment.

The Council of Rheims in 1148, presided over by Eugenius III, did not even speak of this penalty, but simply forbade secular princes to give support or asylum to heretics.[3] We know, moreover, that at this council Éon de l'Étoile was merely sentenced to the seclusion of a monastery.

In fact, the execution of heretics which occurred during the eleventh and twelfth centuries were due to the impulse of the moment. As an historian has remarked: "These heretics were not punished for a crime against the law; for there was no legal crime of heresy and no penalty prescribed. But the men of

---

[1] Cf. Labbe, *Concilia*, vol. ix, col. 1042.

[2] Council of Toulouse, can. 3, Labbe, vol. x, col. 857; Council of Lateran, can. 23, *ibid.*, col. 1008.

[3] Can. 18, Labbe, *Concilia*, vol. x, col. 1113.

the day adopted what they considered a measure of public safety, to put an end to a public danger." [1]

Far from encouraging the people and the princes in their attitude, the Church through her bishops, teachers, and councils continued to declare that she had a horror of bloodshed: *A domo sacerdotis sanguinis questio remota sit*, writes Geroch of Reichersberg.[2] Peter Cantor also insists on the same idea. "Even if they are proved guilty by the judgment of God," he writes, "the Cathari ought not to be sentenced to death, because this sentence is in a way ecclesiastical, being made always in the presence of a priest. If then they are executed, the priest is responsible for their death, for he by whose authority a thing is done is responsible therefor." [3]

Was excommunication to be the only penalty for heresy? Yes, answered Wazo, Leo IX, and the Council of Reims in the middle of the eleventh century. But later on the growth of the evil induced the churchmen of the time to call upon the aid of the civil power. They thought that the Church's excommunication required a temporal sanction. They therefore called upon the princes to banish heretics from their dominions, and to imprison those who refused to be converted. Such was the theory of the twelfth century.

We must not forget, however, that the penalty of imprisonment, which was at first a monastic punishment, had two objects in view: to prevent heretics

---

[1] Julien Havet, *L'hérésie et le bras séculier au moyen âge*, in his *Œuvres*, vol. ii, p. 134.

[2] *De investigatione Antichristi*, lib. i, cap. xlii, *loc. cit.*, pp. 88, 89.

[3] *Verbum abbreviatum*, cap. lxxviii, Migne, P. L., vol. ccv, col. 231.

from spreading their doctrines, and to give them an opportunity of atoning for their sins. In the minds of the ecclesiastical judges, it possessed a penitential, almost a sacramental character. In a period when all Europe was Catholic, it could well supplant exile and banishment, which were the severest civil penalties after the death penalty.

CHAPTER IV

FOURTH PERIOD

FROM GRATIAN TO INNOCENT III

THE INFLUENCE OF THE CANON LAW, AND THE REVIVAL OF THE ROMAN LAW

THE development of the Canon law and the revival of the Roman law could not but exercise a great influence upon the minds of princes and churchmen with regard to the suppression of heresy; in fact, they were the cause of a legislation of persecution, which was adopted by every country of Christendom.

In the beginning of this period, which we date from Gratian,[1] the prosecution of heresy was still carried on, in a more or less irregular and arbitrary fashion, according to the caprice of the reigning sovereign, or the hasty violence of the populace. But from this time forward we shall see it carried on in the name of both the canon and the civil law: *secundum canonicas et legitimas sanctiones*, as a Council of Avignon puts it.[2]

In Germany and France, especially in northern France, the usual punishment was the stake. We need

---

[1] The Decree of Gratian was written about 1140.

[2] This council was held in 1209, d'Achery, *Spicilegium*, in-fol., vol. i, p. 704, col. 1.

not say much of England, for heresy seems to have made but one visit there in 1166. In 1160, a German prince, whose name is unknown, had several Cathari beheaded. Others were burned at Cologne in 1163. The execution of the heretics condemned at Vezelai by the Abbot of Vezelai and several bishops, forms quite a dramatic picture.

When the heretics had been condemned, the Abbot, addressing the crowd, said: "My brethren, what punishment should be inflicted upon those who refuse to be converted?" All replied: "Burn them." "Burn them." Their wishes were carried out. Two abjured their heresy, and were pardoned, the other seven perished at the stake.[1]

Philip, Count of Flanders, was particularly cruel in prosecuting heretics.[2] He had an able auxiliary also in the Archbishop of Rheims, Guillaume aux Blanches-Mains. The chronicle of Anchin tells us that they sent to the stake a great many nobles and people, clerics, knights, peasants, young girls, married women, and widows, whose property they confiscated and shared between them.[3] This occurred in 1183. Some years before, Archbishop Guillaume and his council had sent two heretical women to the stake.[4]

Hugh, Bishop of Auxerre (1183–1206), prosecuted the neo-Manicheans with equal severity; he confis-

---

[1] Hugo Pictav., *Historia Vezeliacensis monasterii*, lib. iv, ad. finem, *Hist. des Gaules*, vol. xii, pp. 343–344.

[2] Raoul de Coggeshall, in *Rerum Britann. medii ævi Scriptores*, ed. Stevenson, p. 122.

[3] Sigeberti, *Continuatio Aquicinctina*, ad. ann. 1183, in the *Mon. Germ. SS.*, vol. vi, p. 421.

[4] Raoul de Coggeshall, *loc. cit.*; *Hist. des Gaules*, vol. xviii, p. 92.

cated the property of some, banished others, and sent several to the stake.

The reign of Philip Augustus was marked by many executions. Eight Cathari were sent to the stake at Troyes in 1200, one at Nevers in 1201, and several others at Braisne-sur-Vesle in 1204. A most famous case was the condemnation of the followers of the heretic, Amaury de Beynes. " Priests, clerics, men and women belonging to the sect, were brought before a council at Paris; they were condemned and handed over to the secular court of King Philip." The king was absent at the time. On his return he had them all burned outside the walls of the city.

In 1163 a council of Tours enacted a decree fixing the punishment of heresy. Of course it had in view chiefly the Cathari of Toulouse and Gascony: " If these wretches are captured," it says, " the Catholic princes are to imprison them and confiscate their property." [1]

This canon was applied probably for the first time at Toulouse in 1178. The Bishop began proceedings against several heretics, among them a rich noble named Pierre Mauran, who was summoned before his tribunal, and condemned to make a pilgrimage to the Holy Land. His property was confiscated, although later on when he professed repentance it was restored to him, on condition that he dismantle the towers of his castles, and pay the Count of Toulouse a fine of five hundred pounds of silver.

In the meantime the Cathari increased with alarming rapidity throughout this region. Count Raymond V (1148–1194), wishing to strike terror into them,

[1] Can. 4, Labbe, *Concilia*, vol. x, col. 1419.

enacted a law which decreed the confiscation of their property, and death. The people of Toulouse quoted this law later on in a letter to King Pedro of Aragon to justify their sending heretics to the stake, and when the followers of Simon de Montfort arrived in southern France, in 1209, they followed the example of Count Raymond by sending heretics to the stake everywhere they went.

The authenticity of this law has been questioned, on account of its unheard-of severity. But Pedro II, King of Aragon and Count of Barcelona, enacted a law in 1197 which was just as terrible. He banished the Waldenses and all other heretics from his dominions, ordering them to depart before Passion Sunday of the following year (March 23, 1198). After that day, every heretic found in the kingdom or the county was to be sent to the stake, and his property confiscated. It is worthy of remark, that in the king's mind the stake was merely a subsidiary penalty.

In enacting this severe law, Pedro of Aragon declared that he was moved by zeal for the public welfare, and "had simply obeyed the canons of the Holy Roman Church." With the exception of the death penalty by the stake, his reference to the canon law is perfectly accurate. Pope Alexander III, who had been present at the Council of Tours in 1163, renewed, at the Lateran Council in 1179, the decrees already enacted against the heretics of central France. He considered the Cathari, the Brabançons, etc., disturbers of the public welfare, and therefore called upon the princes to protect by force of arms their Christian subjects against the outrages of these heretics. The princes were to imprison all heretics and confiscate their property. The Pope granted indulgences to all who carried on this pious work.

In 1184, Pope Lucius III, in union with the Emperor Frederic Barbarossa, adopted at Verona still more vigorous measures. Heretics were to be excommunicated, and then handed over to the secular arm, which was to inflict upon them the punishment they deserved (*animadversio debita*).[1] The Emperor decreed the imperial ban against them.

This imperial ban was, as Ficker has pointed out, a very severe penalty in Italy; for it comprised banishment, the confiscation of the property, and the destruction of the houses of the condemned, public infamy, the inability to hold public office, etc. This is beyond question the penalty the King of Aragon alluded to in his enactment. The penalty of the stake which he added, although in conformity with the Roman law, was an innovation.

The pontificate of Innocent III, which began in 1198, marks a pause in the development of the Church's penal legislation against heresy. Despite his prodigious activity, this Pope never dreamt of enacting new laws, but did his best to enforce the laws then in vogue, and to stimulate the zeal of both princes and magistrates in the suppression of heresy.

Hardly had he ascended the pontifical throne when he sent legates to southern France, and wrote urgent letters full of apostolic zeal to the Archbishops of Auch and Aix, the Bishop of Narbonne, and the King of France. These letters, as well as his instructions to the legates, are similar in tone: " Use against heretics

[1] Canon 27, inserted in the Decretals of Gregory IX, lib. **v, tit.** vii, *De Hæreticis*, cap. ix.

the spiritual sword of excommunication, and if this does not prove effective, use the material sword. The civil laws decree banishment and confiscation; see that they are carried out."[1]

At this time the Cathari were living not only in the cities of Languedoc and Provence, but some had even entered the papal States, *v. g.*, at Orvieto and Viterbo. The Pope himself went to these cities to combat the evil, and at once saw the necessity of enacting special laws against them. They may be read in his letters of March 25, 1199, and September 22, 1207, which form a special code for the use of the princes and the podestà. Heretics were to be branded with infamy; they were forbidden to be electors, to hold public office, to be members of the city councils, to appear in court or testify, to make a will or to receive an inheritance; if officials, all their acts were declared null and void; and finally their property was to be confiscated.

"In the territories subject to our temporal jurisdiction," adds the Pope, "we declare their property confiscated; in other places we order the podestà and the secular princes to do the same, and we desire and command this law enforced under penalty of ecclesiastical censures."[2]

We are not at all surprised at such drastic measures, when we consider the agreement made by Lucius III with Frederic Barbarossa, at Verona. But we wish to call attention to the reasons that Innocent III adduced to justify his severity, on account of the serious consequences they entailed. "The civil law," says

[1] Letters of Innocent III in Migne, P. L., vol. ccxiv–ccxvi.
[2] Letter of March 25, 1199, to the magistrates and people of Viterbo; constitution of September 23, 1207, *Ep.* x, 130.

the Pope, " punishes traitors with confiscation of their property and death; it is only out of kindness that the lives of their children are spared. All the more then should we excommunicate and confiscate the property of those who are traitors to the faith of Jesus Christ; for it is an infinitely greater sin to offend the Divine Majesty than to attack the majesty of the sovereign." [1]

Whether this comparison be justified or not, it is certainly most striking. Later on Frederic II and others will quote it to justify their severity.

The Lateran Council in 1215 made the laws of Innocent III canons of the universal Church; it declared all heretics excommunicated, and delivered them over to the State to receive due punishment. This *animadversio debita* entailed banishment with all its consequences and confiscation. The council also legislated against the abettors of heresy, even if they were princes, and ordered the despoiling of all rulers who neglected to enforce the ecclesiastical law in their domains.[2]

In practice, Innocent III, although very severe towards obdurate heretics, was extremely kind to the ignorant and heretics in good faith. While he banished the Patarins from Viterbo,[3] and razed their houses to the ground, he at the same time protected, against the tyranny of an archpriest of Verona, a society of mystics, the Humiliati, whose orthodoxy was rather doubtful. When, after the massacre of the Albigenses, Pope Innocent was called upon to apply the canon law

[1] Letter of March 25, 1199, to the magistrates of Viterbo, *Ep.* ii, 1.

[2] Labbe, *Concilia*, vol. xi, col. 148–150; *Decretales*, cap. xiii, *De hæreticis*, lib. v, tit. vii.

[3] *Gesta Innocentii*, cap. cxxiii, Migne, P. L., vol. ccxiv, col. clxi.

in the case of Raymond, Count of Toulouse, and to transfer the patrimony of his father to Simon de Montfort, he was the first to draw back from such injustice. Although a framer of severe laws against heresy, he was ready to grant dispensations, when occasion arose.

We must remember also that the laws he enacted were not at all excessive compared with the strict Roman law, or even with the practice then in vogue in France and Germany. It has been justly said: "The laws and letters of Innocent III never once mention the death penalty for heresy. He merely decrees against them banishment, and the confiscation of their property. When he speaks of having recourse to the secular arm, he means simply the force required to carry out the laws of banishment enacted by his penal code. This code, which seems so pitiless to us, was in reality at that time a great improvement in the treatment of heretics. For its special laws prevented the frequent outbreaks of popular vengeance, which punished not only confessed heretics, but also mere suspects." [1]

In fact, the development in the methods of suppressing heresy from the eleventh century, ends with Innocent III in a code that was far more kindly than the cruel customs in vogue at the time.

The death penalty of the stake was common in

---

[1] Luchaire, Innocent III, *et la croisade des Albigeois*, pp. 57, 58. Julien Havet also says: "We must in justice say of Innocent III that, if he did bitterly prosecute heretics, and everywhere put them under the ban, he never demanded the infliction of the death penalty. Ficker has brought this out very clearly." *L'hérésie et le bras séculier*, p. 165, n. 3. For Ficker's view, cf. *op. cit.*, pp. 189–192.

France in the twelfth century, and in the beginning of the thirteenth. Most of the executions were due to the passions of the mob, although the Roman law was in part responsible. Anselm of Lucca and the author of the *Panormia* (Ivo of Chartres?) had copied word for word the fifth law of the title *De Hæreticis* of the Justinian code, under the rubric: *De edicto imperatorum in damnationem hæreticorum*.[1] This law which decreed the death penalty against the Manicheans, seemed strictly applicable to the Cathari, who were regarded at the time as the direct heirs of Manicheism. Gratian, in his Decree, maintained the views of St. Augustine on the penalties of heresy, viz., fine and banishment.[2] But some of his commentators, especially Rufinus, Johannes, Teutonicus, and an anonymous writer whose work is inserted in Huguccio's great *Summa* of the Decree, declared that impenitent heretics might and even ought to be put to death.

These different works appeared before the Lateran Council of 1215.[3] They are a good indication of the mind of the time. We may well ask whether the Archbishop of Rheims, the Count of Flanders, Philip Augustus, Raymond of Toulouse, and Pedro of Aragon, who authorized the use of the stake for heretics, did not think they were following the example of the first Christian emperors. We must, however, admit that there is no direct allusion to the early imperial legislation either in their acts or their writings. Probably

[1] Tanon, *op. cit.*, pp. 453–454.
[2] Decretum, 2 Pars, Causa xxiii, quest. 4, 6, 7.
[3] The collection of Anselm of Lucca is prior to 1080. The *Panormia* was written about the beginning of the twelfth century; the Decree about 1140; the three commentaries were written a little before 1215.

they were more influenced by the customs of the time than by the written law.

As a matter of fact, Gratian, who with St. Augustine mentioned only fine and banishment as the penalties for heresy, was followed for some time. We learn from Benencasa's *Summa* of the Decree that heretics were punished not by death, but by banishment and confiscation of their property.[1]

The Councils of Tours and Lateran also decreed confiscation, but for banishment they substituted imprisonment, a penalty unknown to the Roman law. The Council of Lateran appealed to the authority of St. Leo the Great, to compel Christian princes to prosecute heresy.[2]

From the time of Lucius III, owing to the influence of the lawyers, the two penalties of banishment and confiscation prevailed. Innocent III extended them to the universal Church.

This was undoubtedly a severer penal legislation than that of the preceding age. But, on the other hand, it was an effective barrier against the infliction of the death penalty, which had become so common in many parts of Christendom.

Besides, during this period, the Church used vigorous measures only against obdurate heretics, who were also disturbers of the public peace.[3] They alone were handed over to the secular arm; if they abjured their

---

[1] *Biblioth. Nation.*, Ms. 3892, *Summa* of Benencasa: 41, cap. 23, q. 4, *Non invenitur*.

[2] Canon 27, Labbe, *Concilia*, vol. x, col. 1522; Leonis, *Epist.* xv, ad Turribium, Migne, *Pat. lat.*, vol. liv. col, 679–680.

[3] Innocent III merely condemned to prison in a monastery the heretical abbot of Nevers; cf. letter of June 19, 1199, to a cardinal and a bishop of Paris. *Ep.* ii, 99.

THE INQUISITION

heresy, they were at once pardoned, provided they freely accepted the penance imposed upon them.[1] This kind treatment, it was true, was not to last. It, however, deserves special notice, for the honor of those who preached and practiced it.

[1] Cf. Canon 27 of the Lateran Council (1179), which we have quoted above, and which is inserted in the Decretals of Gregory x, cap. ix, *De hæreticis*, lib. v, tit. vii.

CHAPTER V

The Catharan or Albigensian Heresy—Its Anti-Catholic and Anti-Social Character

While Popes Alexander III, Lucius III, and Innocent III, were adopting such vigorous measures, the Catharan heresy by its rapid increase caused widespread alarm throughout Christendom. Let us endeavor to obtain some insight into its character, before we describe the Inquisition, which was destined to destroy it.

The dominant heresy of the period was the Albigensian or Catharan heresy;[1] it was related to Oriental Manicheism[2] through the Paulicians and the Bogomiles, who professed a dualistic theory on the origin of the world.

In the tenth century, the Empress Theodora, who detested the Paulicians, had one hundred thousand of them massacred; the Emperor Alexis Comnenus (about 1118), persecuted the Bogomiles in like manner. Many, therefore, of both sects went to western Europe, where they finally settled, and began to spread.

As early as 1167, they held a council at St. Felix de Caraman, near Toulouse, under the presidency of one

[1] The heretics called themselves "*Cathari*," or "*the Pure.*" They wished thereby to denote especially their horror of all sexual relations, says the monk Egbert: *Sermones contra Catharos*, in Migne, P. L., cxcv, col. 13.

[2] On the origin of the Manichean heresy, cf. Duchesne, *Histoire ancienne de l'Église*, pp. 555, 556.

of their leaders, Pope or perhaps only Bishop Niketas (Niquinta) of Constantinople. Other bishops of the sect were present: Mark, who had charge of all the churches of Lombardy, Tuscany, and the Marches of Treviso; Robert de Sperone, who governed a church in the north, and Sicard Cellerier, Bishop of the Church of Albi. They appointed Bernard Raymond, Bishop of Toulouse, Guiraud Mercier, Bishop of Carcassonne, and Raymond of Casalis, Bishop of Val d'Aran, in the diocese of Comminges. Such an organization certainly indicates the extraordinary development of the heresy about the middle of the twelfth century.

About the year 1200 its progress was still more alarming. Bonacursus, a Catharan bishop converted to Catholicism, writes about 1190: " Behold the cities, towns and homes filled with these false prophets." [1] Cæsarius, of Heisterbach, tells us that a few years later there were Cathari in about one thousand cities,[2] especially in Lombardy and Languedoc.

There were at least seven to eight hundred of " the Perfected " in Languedoc alone; and to obtain approximately the total number of the sect, we must multiply this number by twenty or even more.[3]

Of course, perfect unity did not exist among the Cathari. The different names by which they were known clearly indicate certain differences of doctrine among them. Some, like the Cathari of Alba and Desenzano, taught with the Paulicians an absolute dualism, affirming that all things created came from

---

[1] *Manifestatio hæresis Catharorum*, in Migne, P. L., vol. cciv, col. 778.

[2] *Dialogi*, Antwerp, 1604, p. 289.

[3] This is Döllinger's estimate, *Beiträge*, vol. i, pp. 212, 213.

two principles, the one essentially good, and the other essentially bad. Two other groups, the Concorrezenses and the Bagolenses, like the ancient Gnostics, held a modified form of dualism; they pretended that the evil spirit had so marred the Creator's work, that matter had become the instrument of evil in the world. Still they agreed with the pronounced dualists in nearly all their doctrines and observances; their few theoretical differences were scarcely appreciable in practice.[1]

Still, contemporary writers called them by different names. In Italy they were confounded with the orthodox Patarins and Arnaldists of Milan; which explains the frequent use of the word *Patareni* in the constitutions of Frederic II, and other documents.

The Arnaldists or Arnoldists and the Speronistæ, were the disciples of Arnold of Brescia, and the heretical Bishop Sperone. Although the chief center of the Cathari in France was Toulouse and not Albi, they were called *Albigeois* (Albigenses), and *Tisserands* (Texerants), because many were weavers by trade; *Arians*, because of their denial of Christ's divinity; *Paulicians*, which was corrupted into *Poplicani*, *Publicani*, *Piphes* and *Piples* (Flanders); *Bulgarians* (*Bulgari*), from their origin, which became in the mouths of the people of *Bugari*, *Bulgri*, and *Bugres*. In fact about 1200, nearly all the heretics of western Europe were considered Cathari.

Catharism was chiefly a negative heresy; it denied the doctrines, hierarchy and worship of the Catholic Church, as well as the essential rights of the State.

---

[1] On the Catharan doctrines, cf. Döllinger's *Beiträge*.

THE INQUISITION 53

These neo-Manicheans denied that the Roman Church represented the Church of Christ. The Popes were not the successors of St. Peter, but rather the successors of Constantine. St. Peter never came to Rome. The relics which were venerated in the Constantinian basilica, were the bones of some one who died in the third century; they were not relics of the Prince of the Apostles. Constantine unfortunately sanctioned this fraud, by conferring upon the Roman pontiff an immense domain, together with the prestige that accompanies temporal authority.[1] How could anyone recognize under the insignia, the purple mantle, and the crown of the successors of St. Sylvester, a disciple of Jesus Christ? Christ had no place where to lay His head, whereas the Popes lived in a palace! Christ rebuked worldly dominion, while the Popes claimed it! What had the Roman curia with its thirst for riches and honors in common with the gospel of Christ? What were these archbishops, primates, cardinals, archdeacons, monks, canons, Dominicans, and Friars Minor but the Pharisees of old! The priests placed heavy burdens upon the faithful people, and they themselves did not touch them with the tips of their fingers; they received tithes from the fields and flocks; they ran after the heritage of widows; all practices which Christ condemned in the Pharisees.

And yet, withal, they dared persecute humble souls who, by their pure life, tried to realize the perfect ideal

[1] The Middle Ages believed firmly in the donation of Constantine. It was, however, questioned by Wetzel, a disciple of Arnold of Brescia, in 1152, in a letter to Frederic Barbarossa, Martène and Durand, *Veterum scriptorum . . . amplissima collectio*, Paris, 1724, vol. ii, col. 554–557.

proposed by Christ! These persecutors were not the true disciples of Jesus. The Roman Church was the woman of the Apocalypse,[1] drunk with the blood of the Saints, and the Pope was Antichrist.

The sacraments of the Church were a mere figment of the imagination. The Cathari made one sacrament out of Baptism, Confirmation, Penance and Eucharist, which they called the *consolamentum;* they denied the real presence of Jesus Christ in the Eucharist, and they repudiated marriage.

Baptism of water was to them an empty ceremony, as valueless as the baptism of John. Christ had undoubtedly said: "Unless a man be born again of water and the Holy Ghost, he cannot enter into the Kingdom of God."[2] But the acts of the Apostles proved that baptism was a mere ceremony, for they declared that the Samaritans, although baptized, had not thereby received the Holy Spirit, by Whom alone the soul is purified from sin.[3]

The Catholic Church also erred greatly in teaching infant baptism. As their faculties were undeveloped, infants could not receive the Holy Spirit. The Cathari —at least to the middle of the thirteenth century— did not confer the *consolamentum* upon newly born infants. According to them, the Church could only abandon these little ones to their unhappy destiny. If they died, they were either forever lost, or, as others taught, condemned to undergo successive incarnations, until they received the *consolamentum*, which classed them with "the Perfected."

---

[1] Apoc. vii, 3, 18.
[2] John iii. 5.
[3] Acts i. 5; viii. 14–17.

It was preposterous to imagine that Christ wished to change bread and wine into His Body in the Eucharist. The Cathari considered transubstantiation as the worst of abominations, since matter, in every form, was the work of the Evil Spirit. They interpreted the Gospel texts in a figurative sense: " This is My Body," they said, simply means: " This represents My Body," thus anticipating the teaching of Carlstadt and Zwingli. They all agreed in denouncing Catholics for daring to claim that they really partook of the Body of Christ, as if Christ could enter a man's stomach, to say nothing worse; or as if Christ would expose Himself to be devoured by rats and mice.

The Cathari, denying the real presence of Jesus Christ in the Eucharist, rejected the sacrifice of the Mass. God, according to them, repudiated all sacrifices. Did He not teach us through His prophet Osee: " I desire mercy and not sacrifice." [1]

The Lord's Supper which the Apostles ate so often was something altogether different from the Roman Mass. They knew nothing of sacerdotal vestments, stone altars with shining candelabra, incense, hymns, and chantings. They did not worship in an immense building called a church—a word which should be applied exclusively to the assembly of the saints.

The Cathari, in their hatred of Catholic piety, railed in the most abusive language against the veneration of images, and especially of the cross. The images and statues of the saints were to them nothing but idols, which ought to be destroyed. The cross on which Jesus died should be hated rather than rever-

---

[1] Osee vi. 6.

enced. Some of them, moreover, denied that Jesus had been really crucified; they held that a demon died, or feigned to die in His stead. Even those who believed in the reality of the Saviour's crucifixion made this very belief a reason for condemning the veneration of the cross. What man is there, they said, who could see a loved one, for example a father, die upon a cross, and not feel ever after a deep hatred of this instrument of torture? The cross, therefore, should not be reverenced, but despised, insulted and spat upon. One of them even said: "I would gladly hew the cross to pieces with an axe, and throw it into the fire to make the pot boil."

Not only were the Cathari hostile to the Church and her divine worship, but they were also in open revolt against the State, and its rights.

The feudal society rested entirely upon the oath of fealty (*jusjurandum*), which was the bond of its strength and solidity.

According to the Cathari, Christ taught that it was sinful to take an oath, and that the speech of every Christian should be yes, yes; no, no.[1] Nothing, therefore, could induce them to take an oath.

The authority of the State, even when Christian, appeared to them, in certain respects, very doubtful. Had not Christ questioned Peter, saying: "What is thy opinion, Simon? The kings of the earth, of whom do they receive tribute or custom? of their own children, or of strangers?" Peter replied: "Of strangers." Jesus said to him: "Then are the children free (of every obligation)."[2]

[1] Matt. v. 37; James v. 12.
[2] Matt. xvii. 24, 25.

The Cathari quoted these words to justify their refusal of allegiance to princes. Were they not disciples of Christ, whom the truth had made free? Some of them not only disputed the lawfulness of taxation, but went so far as to condone stealing, provided the thief had done no injury to " Believers." [1]

Some of the Cathari admitted the authority of the State, but denied its right to inflict capital punishment. "It is not God's will," said Pierre Garsias, "that human justice condemn any one to death;" and when one of the Cathari became consul of Toulouse, he wrote to remind him of this absolute law. But the *Summa contra hæreticos* asserts: "all the Catharan sects taught that the public prosecution of crime was unjust, and that no man had a right to administer justice;" [2] a teaching which denied the State's right to punish.

The Cathari interpreted literally the words of Christ to Peter: "All that take the sword shall perish with the sword," [3] and applied the commandment *Non occides* absolutely. "In no instance," they said, "has one the right to kill another;" [4] neither the internal welfare of a country, nor its external interests can justify murder. War is never lawful. The soldier defending his country is just as much a murderer as the most common criminal. It was not any special

[1] Contrary to the Catholic teaching, the Cathari absolved those who stole from "non-believers," without obliging them to make restitution. Döllinger, *Beiträge*, vol. ii, pp. 248, 249; cf. pp. 245, 246.

[2] *Summa contra hæreticos.* ed. Douais, p. 133, Moneta, *op. cit.*, p. 513.

[3] Matt. xxvi. 52.

[4] Cf. Döllinger, *Beiträge*, vol. ii, p. 199.

aversion to the crusades, but their horror of war in general, that made the Cathari declare the preachers of the crusades murderers.

These anti-Catholic, anti-patriotic, and anti-social theories were only the negative side of Catharism. Let us now ascertain what they substituted for the Catholic doctrines they denied.

Catharism, as we have already hinted, was a hodgepodge of pagan dualism and Gospel teaching, given to the world as a sort of reformed Christianity.

Human souls, spirits fallen from heaven into a material body which is the work of the Evil Spirit, were subject on this earth to a probation, which was ended by Christ, or rather by the Holy Spirit. They were set free by the imposition of hands, the secret of which had been committed to the true Church by the disciples of Jesus.

This Church had its rulers, the Bishops, and its members who are called "the Perfected," "the Consoled," and "the Believers."

We need not dwell upon the episcopate of the Catharan hierarchy. Suffice it to say that the Bishop was always surrounded by three dignitaries, the *Filius Major*, the *Filius Minor*, and the Deacon. The Bishop had charge of the most important religious ceremonies: the imposition of hands for the initiation or *consolamentum*, the breaking of bread which replaced the Eucharist, and the liturgical prayers such as the recitation of the Lord's Prayer. When he was absent, the *Filius Major*, the *Filius Minor*, or the Deacon took his place. It was seldom, however, that these dignitaries traveled alone; the Bishop was always accompanied by his Deacon, who served as his *socius*.

One joined the Church by promising (the *Convenenza*) to renounce the Catholic faith, and to receive the Catharan initiation (the *consolamentum*), at least at the hour of death. This was the first step on the road to perfection. Those who agreed to make it were called " the Believers." Their obligations were few. They were not bound to observe the severe Catharan fasts, which we will mention later on. They could live in the world like other mortals, and were even allowed to eat meat and to marry. Their chief duty was " to venerate " " the Perfected," each time they entered their presence. They genuflected, and prostrated themselves three times, saying each time as they rose, " Give us your blessing; " the third time they added: " Good Christians, give us God's blessing and yours; pray God that He preserve us from an evil death, and bring us to a good end! " The Perfected replied: " Receive God's blessing and ours; may God bless you, preserve you from an evil death, and bring you to a good end." If these heretics were asked why they made others venerate them in this manner, they replied that the Holy Spirit dwelling within them gave them the right to such homage. The Believers were always required to pay this extraordinary mark of respect. In fact it was a *sine qua non* of their being admitted to the *Convenenza*.

The *Convenenza* was not merely an external bond, uniting " the Believers " and " the Perfected," but it was also an earnest of eternal salvation. It assured the future destiny of " the Believers; " it gave them the right to receive the *consolamentum* on their deathbed. This remitted all the sins of their life. Only one thing could deprive them of " this good end, " viz., the absence of one of the Perfected, who **alone** could lay hands upon them.

Those who died without the Catharan *consolamentum* were either eternally lost, or condemned to begin life anew with another chance of becoming one of " the good men." These transmigrations of the soul were rather numerous. The human soul did not always pass directly from the body of a man into the body of another man. It occasionally entered into the bodies of animals, like the ox and the ass. The Cathari were wont to tell the story of " a good Christian," one of " the Perfected," who remembered, in a previous existence as a horse, having lost his shoe in a certain place between two stones, as he was running swiftly under his master's spur. When he became a man he was curious enough to hunt for it, and he found it in the self-same spot. Such humiliating transmigrations were undoubtedly rather rare. A woman named Sybil, " a Believer " and later on one of " the Perfected," remembered having been a queen in a prior existence.

What the *Convenenza* promised, the Catharan initiation or *consolamentum* gave; the first made " Believers," and predisposed souls to sanctity; the second made " the Perfected," and conferred sanctity with all its rights and prerogatives.

The *consolamentum* required a preparation which we may rightly compare with the catechumenate of the early Christians.

This probation usually lasted one year. It consisted in an honest attempt to lead the life of "the Perfected," and chiefly in keeping their three " lents," abstaining from meat, milk-food and eggs. It was therefore called the time of abstinence (*abstinentia*). One of " the Perfected" was appointed by the Church to report upon the life of the postulant, who daily had to venerate his superior, according to the Catharan rite.

After this probation, came the ceremony of "the delivery" (*traditio*) of the Lord's Prayer. A number of "the Perfected" were always present. The highest dignitary, the Bishop or "the Ancient," made the candidate a lengthy speech, which has come down to us:

"Understand," he said, "that when you appear before the Church of God you are in the presence of the Father, the Son and the Holy Spirit, as the Scriptures prove," etc. Then, having repeated the Lord's Prayer to "the Believer" word for word, and having explained its meaning, he continued: "We deliver to you this holy prayer, that you may receive it from us, from God, and from the Church, that you may have the right to say it all your life, day and night, alone and in company, and that you may never eat or drink without first saying it. If you omit it, you must do penance." The Believer replied: "I receive it from you and from the Church."[1]

After these words came the *Abrenuntiatio*. At the Catholic baptism, the catechumen renounced Satan, with his works and pomps. According to the Catharan ritual, the Catholic Church was Satan.

"The Perfected" said to the Believer: "Friend, if you wish to be one of us, you must renounce all the doctrines of the Church of Rome;" and he replied: "I do renounce them."

—Do you renounce that cross made with chrism upon your breast, head, and shoulders?

[1] Clédat, *Rituel Cathare*, pp. xi–xv.

—I do renounce it.

—Do you believe that the water of Baptism is efficacious for salvation?

—No, I do not believe it.

—Do you renounce the veil, which the priest placed upon your head, after you were baptized?

—I do renounce it.[1]

Again the Bishop addressed " the Believer " to impress upon him the new duties involved in his receiving the Holy Spirit. Those who were present prayed God to pardon the candidate's sins, and then venerated " the Perfected " (the ceremony of the *Parcia*). After the Bishop's prayer, " May God bless thee, make thee a good Christian, and grant thee a good end," the candidate made a solemn promise faithfully to fulfill the duties he had learned during his *probatio*. The words of his promise are to be found in Sacconi: " I promise to devote my life to God and to the Gospel, never to lie or swear, never to touch a woman, never to kill an animal, never to eat meat, eggs or milk-food; never to eat anything but fish and vegetables, never to do anything without first saying the Lord's Prayer, never to eat, travel, or pass the night without a *socius*. If I fall into the hands of my enemies or happen to be separated from my *socius*, I promise to spend three days without food or drink. I will never take off my clothes on retiring, nor will I deny my faith even when threatened with death." The ceremony of the *Parcia* was then repeated.

Then, according to the ritual, " the Bishop takes the book (the New Testament), and places it upon the

[1] Sacconi, *Summa de Catharis*, in Martène and Durand, *Thesaurus novus anecdotorum*, vol. v, p. 1776.

head of the candidate," while the other " good men " present impose hands upon him, saying: " Holy Father, accept this servant of yours in all righteousness, and send your grace and your Spirit upon him." The Holy Spirit was then supposed to descend, and the ceremony of the *consolamentum* was finished; " the Believer " had become one of " the Perfected."

However, before the assembly dispersed, " the Perfected " proceeded to carry out two other ceremonies: the vesting and the kiss of peace.

" While their worship was tolerated," writes an historian,[1] " they gave their new brother a black garment; but in times of persecution they did not wear it, for fear of betraying themselves to the officials of the Inquisition. In the thirteenth century, in southern France, they were known by the linen or flaxen belt, which the men wore over their shirts, and the women wore *cordulam cinctam ad carnem nudam subtus mamillas*. They resembled the cord or scapular that the Catholic tertiaries wore to represent the habit of the monastic order to which they belonged. They were therefore called *hæretici vestiti*, which became a common term for " the Perfected."

" The last ceremony was the kiss of peace, which 'the Perfected' gave their new brother, by kissing him twice (on the mouth), *bis in ore ex transverso*. He in turn kissed the one nearest him, who passed on the *pax* to all present. If the recipient was a woman, the minister gave her the *pax* by touching her shoulder with the book of the gospels, and his elbow with hers. She transmitted this symbolic kiss in the same manner

[1] Jean Guiraud, *Le consolamentum ou initiation cathare, loc. cit.*, p. 134.

to the one next to her, if he was a man. After a last fraternal embrace, they all congratulated the new brother, and the assembly dispersed."

The promises made by this new member of "the Perfected" were not all equally hard to keep. As far as positive duties were concerned, there were but three: the daily recitation of the Lord's Prayer, the breaking of bread, and the *Apparellamentum*.

Only "the Perfected" were allowed to recite the Lord's Prayer. The Cathari explained the esoteric character of this prayer by that passage in the Apocalypse which speaks of the one hundred and forty-four thousand elect who follow the Lamb whithersoever He goeth, and who sing a hymn which only virgins can sing.[1] This hymn was the *Pater Noster*. Married people, therefore, and consequently "the Believers," could not repeat it without profanation. But "the Perfected" were obliged to say it every day, especially before meals.[2]

They blessed the bread without making the sign of the cross.

This "breaking of bread" replaced the Eucharist. They thought in this way to reproduce the Lord's Supper, while they repudiated all the ceremonies of the Catholic Mass. "The Believers" partook of this blessed bread when they sat at the table with "the Perfected," and they were wont to carry some of it home to eat from time to time.

[1] Apoc. xiv. 1–4.
[2] The Perfected had to live with a *socius* who blessed his food, while he in turn had to bless the food of his companion. If he separated from his *socius*, he had to do without food and drink for three days. This frequently happened when they were arrested and cast into prison.

Some attributed to it a wonderful sanctifying power, and believed that if at their death none of "the Perfected" were present to administer the *consolamentum*, this "bread of the holy prayer" would itself ensure their salvation. They were therefore very anxious to keep some of it on hand; and we read of "the Believers" of Languedoc having some sent them from Lombardy, when they were no longer able to communicate with their persecuted brethren.

It was usually distributed to all present during the *Apparellamentum*. This was the solemn monthly reunion of all the Cathari, "the Believers" and "the Perfected." All present confessed their sins, no matter how slight, although only a general confession was required. As a rule the Deacon addressed the assembly, which closed with the *Parcia* and the kiss of peace: *osculantes sese invicem ex transverso*.

There was nothing very hard in this; on the contrary, it was the consoling side of their life. But their rigorous laws of fasting and abstinence constituted a most severe form of mortification.

"The Perfected" kept three Lents a year; the first from St. Brice's day (November 13) till Christmas; the second from Quinquagesima Sunday till Easter; the third from Pentecost to the feast of Saints Peter and Paul. They called the first and last weeks of these Lents the strict weeks (*septimana stricta*), because during them they fasted on bread and water every day, whereas the rest of the time they fasted only three days out of the seven. Besides these special penitential seasons, they observed the same rigorous fast three days a week all during the year, unless they were sick or were traveling.[1]

[1] Bernard Gui, *Practica inquisitionis*, p. 239.

These heretics were known everywhere by their fasting and abstinence. "They are good men," it was said, "who live holy lives, fasting three days a week, and never eating meat." [1]

They never ate meat, in fact, and this law of abstinence extended, as we have seen, to eggs, cheese, and everything which was the result of animal propagation. They were allowed, however, to eat cold-blooded animals like fish, because of the strange idea they had of their method of propagation.

One of the results, or rather one of the causes of their abstinence from meat, was the absolute respect they had for animal life in general. We have seen that they admitted metempsychosis. According to their belief, the body of an ox or an ass might be the dwelling place of a human soul. To kill these animals, therefore, was a crime equivalent to murder. "For that reason," says Bernard Gui, "they never kill an animal or a bird; for they believe that in animals and birds dwell the souls of men, who died without having been received into their sect by the imposition of hands." [2] This was also one of the signs by which they could be known as heretics. We read of them being condemned at Goslar and elsewhere for having refused to kill and eat a chicken.

Their most extraordinary mortification was the law of chastity, as they understood and practiced it. They had a great horror of Christian marriage, and endeavored to defend their views by the Scriptures. Had not Christ said: "Whosoever shall look on

---

[1] Douais, *Les manuscrits du château de Merville*, in the *Annales du Midi*, 1890, p. 185.

[2] *Practica Inquisitionis*, p. 240.

a woman to lust after her, hath already committed adultery with her in his heart;"[1] *i. e.*, was he not guilty of a crime? "The children of this world marry," He says again, "and are given in marriage; but they that shall be accounted worthy of that world and of the resurrection from the dead, shall neither be married, nor take wives."[2] "It is good," says St. Paul, "for a man not to touch a woman."[3]

The Cathari interpreted these texts literally, and when their opponents cited other texts of Scripture which plainly taught the sacred character of Christian marriage, they at once interpreted them in a spiritual or symbolic sense. The only legitimate marriage in their eyes was the union of the Bishop with the Church, or the union of the soul with the Holy Spirit by the ceremony of the *consolamentum*.

They condemned absolutely all marital relations. That was the sin of Adam and Eve. Pierre Garsias taught at Toulouse that the forbidden fruit of the Garden of Eden was simply carnal pleasure.

One of the purposes of marriage is the begetting of children. But the propagation of the human species is plainly the work of the Evil Spirit. A woman with child is a woman possessed of the devil. "Pray God," said one of "the Perfected" to the wife of a Toulouse lumber merchant, "pray God that He deliver you from the devil within you." The greatest evil that could befall a woman was to die *enceinte;* for being in the state of impurity and in the power of Satan, she could not be saved. We read of the Cathari saying this to

---

[1] Matt. v. 28.
[2] Luke xx. 34, 35.
[3] I Corinth. vii. 1, 7.

Peirona de la Caustra: *quod si decederet prægnans non posset salvari*.

Marriage, because it made such a condition possible, was absolutely condemned. Bernard Gui thus resumes the teaching of the Cathari on this point: "They condemn marriage absolutely; they maintain that it is a perpetual state of sin; they deny that a good God can institute it. They declare the marital relation as great a sin as incest with one's mother, daughter, or sister." And this is by no means a calumnious charge. The language which Bernard Gui attributes to these heretics was used by them on every possible occasion. They were unable to find words strong enough to express their contempt for marriage. "Marriage," they said, "is nothing but licentiousness; marriage is merely prostitution." In their extreme hatred, they even went so far as to prefer open licentiousness to it, saying: "Cohabitation with one's wife is a worse crime than adultery." One might be inclined to think that this was merely an extravagant outburst; but, on the contrary, they tried to defend this view by reason. Licentiousness, they argued, was a temporary thing, to which a man gave himself up only in secret; he might in time become ashamed of it, repent and renounce it entirely. The married state, on the contrary, caused no shame whatever; men never thought of renouncing it, because they did not dream of the wickedness it entailed: *quia magis publice et sine verecundia peccatum fiebat*.

No one, therefore, was admitted to the *consolamentum* unless he had renounced all marital relations. In this case, the woman "gave her husband to God, and to the good men." It often happened, too, that women, moved by the preaching of "the Perfected," condemned their unconverted husbands to an enforced celibacy. This was one of the results of the neo-Manichean teachings.

Moreover, they carried their principles so far as to consider it a crime even to touch a woman.

They forbade a man to sit next to a woman except in case of necessity. "If a woman touches you," said Pierre Autier, " you must fast three days on bread and water; and if you touch a woman, you must fast nine days on the same diet." At the ceremony of the *consolamentum*, the Bishop who imposed hands on the future sister took great care not to touch her, even with the end of his finger; to avoid doing so, he always covered the postulant with a veil.

But in times of persecution, this over-scrupulous caution was calculated to attract public attention. "The Perfected" (men and women) lived together, pretending that they were married, so that they would not be known as heretics. It was their constant care, however, to avoid the slightest contact. This caused them at times great inconvenience. While traveling, they shared the same bed, the better to avoid suspicion. But they slept with their clothes on, and thus managed to follow out the letter of the law: *tamen induti ita quod unus alium in nuda carne non tangebat.*

Many Catholics were fully persuaded that this pretended love of purity was merely a cloak to hide the grossest immorality. But while we may admit that many of "the Perfected" did actually violate their promise of absolute chastity, we must acknowledge that, as a general rule, they did resist temptation, and preferred death to what they considered impurity.

Many who feared that they might give way in a moment of weakness to the temptations of a corrupt nature, sought refuge in suicide, which was called the *endura*. There were two forms for the sick heretic, suffocation and fasting. The candidate for death was asked whether he desired to be a martyr or a confessor. If he chose to be a martyr, they placed a handkerchief or a pillow over his mouth, until he died of suffocation. If he preferred to be a confessor, he remained without food or drink, until he died of starvation.

The Cathari believed that " the Believers," who asked for the *consolamentum* during sickness, would not keep the laws of their new faith, if they happened to get well. Therefore, to safeguard them against apostasy, they were strongly urged to make their salvation certain by the *endura*. A manuscript of the Register of the Inquisition of Carcassonne, for instance, tells us of a Catharan minister who compelled a sick woman to undergo the *endura*, after he had conferred upon her the Holy Spirit. He forbade any one " to give her the least nourishment . . . and as a matter of fact no food or drink was given her that night or the following day, lest perchance she might be deprived of the benefit of the *consolamentum*.

One of " the Perfected," named Raymond Belhot, congratulated a mother whose daughter he had just " consoled," and ordered her not to give the sick girl anything to eat or drink until he returned, even though she requested it. "If she asks me for it," said the mother, " I will not have the heart to refuse her." " You must refuse her," said " the good man," " or else cause great injury to her soul." From that moment the girl neither ate nor drank; in fact she did not ask for any nourishment. She died the next Saturday.

About the middle of the thirteenth century, when the Cathari began to give the *consolamentum* to infants, they were often cruel enough to make them undergo the *endura*. "One would think," says an historian of the time, "that the world had gone back to those hateful days when unnatural mothers sacrificed their children to Moloch."

It sometimes happened that the parents of "the consoled" withstood more or less openly the cruelty of " the Perfected."

When this happened, some of "the Perfected" remained in the house of the sick person, to see that their murderous prescriptions were obeyed to the letter. Or if this was impossible, they had "the consoled" taken to the house of some friend, where they could readily carry out their policy of starvation.

But as a general rule the "heretics" submitted to the *endura* of their own free will. Raymond Isaure tells us of a certain Guillaume Sabatier who began the *endura* in a retired villa, immediately after his initiation; he starved himself to death in seven weeks. A woman named Gentilis died of the *endura* in six or seven days. A woman of Coustaussa, who had separated from her husband, went to Saverdum to receive the *consolamentum*. She at once began the *endura* at Ax, and died after an absolute fast of about twelve weeks. A certain woman named Montaliva submitted to the *endura;* during it "she ate nothing whatever, but drank some water; she died in six weeks."[1] This case gives us some idea of this terrible practice;

[1] Ms. 609, of the library of Toulouse, fol. 28.

we see that they were sometimes allowed to drink water, which explains the extraordinary duration of some of these suicidal fasts.

Some of the Cathari committed suicide in other ways. A woman of Toulouse named Guillemette first began to subject herself to the *endura* by frequent blood letting; then she tried to weaken herself more by taking long baths; finally she drank poison, and as death did not come quickly enough, she swallowed pounded glass to perforate her intestines.[1] Another woman opened her veins in the bath.[2]

Such methods of suicide were exceptional, although the *endura* itself was common, at least among the Cathari of Languedoc. " Every one," says a trustworthy historian, " who reads the acts of the tribunals of the Inquisition of Toulouse and Carcassonne must admit that the *endura*, voluntary or forced, put to death more victims than the stake or the Inquisition."

Catharism, therefore, was a serious menace to the Church, to the State, and to society.

Without being precisely a Christian heresy, its customs, its hierarchy, and above all its rites of initiation —which we have purposely explained in detail—gave it all the appearance of one. It was really an imitation and a caricature of Christianity. Some of its practices were borrowed from the primitive Christians, as some historians have proved.[3] That in itself would justify the Church in treating its followers as heretics.

---

[1] Ms. 609, of Toulouse, fol. 33.
[2] *Ibid.*, fol. 70.
[3] Jean Guirard, *Le consolamentum ou initiation cathare*, in *Questions d'histoire*, p. 145 seq.

THE INQUISITION

Besides, the Church merely acted in self-defense. The Cathari tried their best to destroy her by attacking her doctrines, her hierarchy, and her apostolic character. If their false teachings had prevailed, disturbing as they did the minds of the people, the Church would have perished.

The princes, who did not concern themselves with these heretics while they merely denied the teachings of the Church, at last found themselves attacked just as vigorously. The Catharan absolute rejection of the oath of fealty was calculated to break the bond that united subjects to their suzerain lords, and at one blow to destroy the whole edifice of feudalism. And even granting that the feudal system could cease to exist without dragging down in its fall all form of government, how could the State provide for the public welfare, if she did not possess the power to punish criminals, as the Cathari maintained?

But the great unpardonable crime of Catharism was its attempt to destroy the future of humanity by its *endura*, and its abolition of marriage. It taught that the sooner life was destroyed the better. Suicide, instead of being considered a crime, was a means of perfection. To beget children was considered the height of immorality. To become one of "the Perfected," which was the only way of salvation, the husband must leave his wife, and the wife her husband. The family must cease to exist, and all men were urged to form a great religious community, vowed to the most rigorous chastity. If this ideal had been realized, the human race would have disappeared from the earth in a few years. Can any one imagine more immoral and more anti-social teaching?

The Catholic Church has been accused of setting up a similar ideal. This is a gross calumny. For while Catharism made chastity a *sine qua non* of salvation, and denounced marriage as something infamous and criminal, the Church merely counsels virginity to an élite body of men and women in whom she recognizes the marks of a special vocation, according to the teaching of the Savior, "He that can take, let him take it." *Qui potest capere capiat.*[1] She endeavors at the same time to uphold the sacrament of marriage, declaring it a holy state, in which the majority of mankind is to work out its salvation.

There is consequently no parity whatever between the two societies and their teachings. In bitterly prosecuting the Cathari, the Church truly acted for the public good. The State was bound to aid her by force, unless it wished to perish herself with all the social order. This explains and to a certain degree justifies the combined action of Church and State in suppressing the Catharan heresy.

[1] Matt. xix. 11, 12.

CHAPTER VI

FIFTH PERIOD

GREGORY IX AND FREDERIC II

THE ESTABLISHMENT OF THE MONASTIC INQUISITION

THE penal system codified by Innocent III was rather liberally interpreted in France and Italy. In order to make the French law agree with it, an oath was added to the coronation service from the time of Louis IX, whereby the King swore to exterminate, *i. e.*, banish all heretics from his kingdom. We are inclined to interpret in this sense the laws of Louis VIII (1226) and Louis IX (April, 1228), for the south of France. The words referring to the punishment of heretics are a little vague: "Let them be punished," says Louis VIII, "with the punishment they deserve." "*Animadversione debita puniantur*. The other penalties specified are infamy and confiscation; in a word, all the consequences of banishment."[1]

Louis IX re-enacted this law in the following terms· "We decree that our barons and magistrates . . . do their duty in prosecuting heretics." "*De ipsis festinanter faciant quod debebunt.*"[2] These words in them-

---
[1] *Ordonnances des roys de France*, vol. xii, pp. 319, 320.
[2] *Ibid.*, vol. i, p. 51; Labbe, *Concilia*, vol. vii, col. 171.

selves are not very clear, and, if we were to interpret them by the customs of a few years later, we might think that they referred to the death penalty, even the stake; but comparing them with similar expressions used by Lucius III and Innocent III, we see that they imply merely the penalty of banishment.

However, a canon of the Council of Toulouse in 1229 seems to make the meaning of these words clear, at least for the future. It decreed that all heretics and their abettors are to be brought to the nobles and the magistrates to receive due punishment, *ut animadversione debita puniantur*. But it adds that " heretics, who, *through fear of death* or any other cause, except their own free will, return to the faith, are to be imprisoned by the bishop of the city to do penance, that they may not corrupt others;" the bishop is to provide for their needs out of the property confiscated.[1] *The fear of death* here seems to imply that the *animadversione debita* meant the death penalty. That would prove the elasticity of the formula. At first it was a legal penalty which custom interpreted to mean banishment and confiscation; later on it meant chiefly the death penalty; and finally it meant solely the penalty of the stake. At any rate, this canon of the Council of Toulouse must be kept in mind; for we will soon see Pope Gregory IX quoting it.

In Italy, Frederic II promulgated on November 22, 1220, an imperial law which, in accordance with the pontifical decree of March 25, 1199, and the Lateran Council of 1215, condemned heretics to every form of banishment, to perpetual infamy, together with the confiscation of their property, and the annulment of

[1] D'Achery, *Spicilegium*, in-fol., vol. i, p. 711.

THE INQUISITION

all their civil acts and powers. It is evident that the emperor was influenced by Innocent III, for, having declared that the children of heretics could not inherit their father's property, he adds a phrase borrowed from the papal decree of 1199, viz., "that to offend the divine majesty was a far greater crime than to offend the majesty of the emperor."[1]

This at once put heresy on a par with treason, and consequently called for a severer punishment than the law actually decreed. We will soon see others draw the logical conclusion from the emperor's comparison, and enact the death penalty for heresy.

The legates of Pope Honorius were empowered to introduce the canonical and imperial legislation into the statutes of the Italian cities, which hitherto had not been at all anxious to take any measures whatever against heretics. They succeeded in Bergamo, Piacenza, and Mantua in 1221; and in Brescia in 1225. In 1226, the emperor himself ordered the podestà of Pavia to banish all heretics from the city limits. About the year 1230, therefore, it was the generally accepted law throughout all Italy (recall what we have said above about Faenza, Florence, etc.) to banish all heretics, confiscate their property, and demolish their houses.

Two years had hardly elapsed when, through the joint efforts of Frederic II and Gregory IX, the death penalty of the stake was substituted for banishment; Guala, a Dominican, seems to have been the prime mover in bringing about this change.

Frederic II, influenced by the jurists who were reviving the old Roman law, promulgated a law for Lom-

[1] *Monum. Germaniæ, Leges*, sect. iv, vol. ii, pp. 107-109.

bardy in 1224, which condemned heretics to the stake, or at least to have their tongues cut out.¹ This penalty of the stake was common—if not legal—in Germany. For instance, we read of the people of Strasburg burning about eighty heretics about the year 1212,² and we could easily cite other similar executions.³ The emperor, therefore, merely brought the use of the stake from Germany into Italy. Indeed it is very doubtful whether this law was in operation before 1230.

But in that year, Guala, the Dominican, who had become Bishop of Brescia, used his authority to enact for his episcopal city the most severe laws against heresy. The podestà of the city had to swear that he would prosecute heretics as Manicheans and traitors, according to both the canon and the civil law, especially in view of Frederic's law of 1224. Innocent III's comparison between heretics and traitors, and between the Cathari and the Manicheans, now bore fruit. Traitors deserved the death penalty, while the old Roman law sent the Manicheans to the stake; accordingly Guala maintained that all heretics deserved the stake.

Pope Gregory IX adopted this stern attitude, probably under the influence of the Bishop of Brescia, with whom he was in frequent correspondence.⁴ The imperial law of 1224 was inscribed in 1230 or 1231 upon the papal register, where it figures as number 103

---

[1] A Constitution sent to the Archbishop of Magdeburg, in the *Mon. Germ., Leges*, sect. iv, vol. ii, p. 126.

[2] *Annales Marbacenses*, ad ann. 1215, in the *Mon. Germ. SS.*, vol. xvii, p. 174.

[3] Cf. Julien Havet, *op. cit.*, pp. 143, 144.

[4] Gregory IX was four years Pope before he enacted these new laws.

of the fourth year of Gregory's pontificate. The Pope then tried to enforce it, beginning with the city of Rome. He enacted a law in February, 1231, ordering, as the Council of Toulouse had done in 1229, heretics condemned by the Church to be handed over to the secular arm, to receive the punishment they deserved, *animadversio debita*. All who abjured and accepted a fitting penance were to be imprisoned for life, without prejudice to the other penalties for heresy, such as confiscation.[1]

About the same time, Annibale, the Senator of Rome, established the new jurisprudence of the Church in the eternal city. Every year, on taking office, the Senator was to banish (*diffidare*) all heretics. All who refused to leave the city were, eight days after their condemnation, to receive the punishment they deserved. The penalty, *animadversio debita*, is not specified, as if every one knew what was meant.

Inasmuch as repentant heretics were imprisoned for life, it seems certain that the severer penalty reserved for obstinate heretics must have been the death penalty of the stake, for that was the mode of punishment decreed by the imperial law of 1224, which had just been copied on the registers of the papal chancery. But we are not left to mere conjecture. In February, 1231, a number of Patarins were arrested in Rome; those who refused to abjure were sent to the stake, while those who did abjure were sent to Monte Cassino and Cava to do penance. This case tells us instantly how we are to interpret the *animadversio debita* of contemporary documents.

---

[1] Cap ii, *Mon. Germ.*, *Leges*, sect. iv, vol. ii, p. 196.

Frederic II exercised an undeniable influence over Gregory IX, and the Pope in turn influenced the emperor. Gregory wrote denouncing the many heretics who swarmed throughout the kingdom of Sicily (the two Sicilies), especially in Naples and Aversa, urging him to prosecute them with vigor. Frederic obeyed. He was then preparing his Sicilian Code, which appeared at Amalfi in August, 1231. The first law, *Inconsutilem tunicam*, was against heretics. The emperor did not have to consult any one about the penalty to be decreed against heresy; he had merely to copy his own law, enacted in Lombardy in 1224. This new law declared heresy a crime against society on a par with treason, and liable to the same penalty. And that the law might not be a dead letter for lack of accusers, the state officials were commanded to prosecute it just as they would any other crime. This was in reality the beginning of the Inquisition. All suspects were to be tried by an ecclesiastical tribunal, and if, being declared guilty, they refuse to abjure, they were to be burned in the presence of the people.[1]

Once started on the road to severity, Frederic II did not stop. To aid Gregory IX in suppressing heresy, he enacted at Ravenna, in 1237, an imperial law condemning all heretics to death.[2] The kind of death was not indicated. But every one knew that the common German custom of burning heretics at the stake had now become the law. For by three previous laws, May 14, 1238, June 26, 1238, and February 22, 1239, the emperor had declared that the

[1] *Constitut. Sicil.*, i, 3, in Eymeric, *Directorium inquisitorum* Appendix, p. 14.
[2] *Mon. Germ.*, *Leges*, sect. iv, vol. ii, p. 196.

THE INQUISITION 81

Sicilian Code and the law of Ravenna were binding upon all his subjects; the law of June 26, 1238, merely promulgated these other laws throughout the kingdom of Arles and Vienne. Henceforth all uncertainty was at an end. The legal punishment for heretics throughout the empire was death at the stake.

Gregory IX did not wait for these laws to be enacted to carry out his intentions.

As early as 1231 he tried to have the cities of Italy and Germany adopt the civil and canonical laws in vogue at Rome against heresy, and he was the first to inaugurate that particular method of prosecution, the permanent tribunal of the Inquisition.

We possess some of the letters which he wrote in June, 1231, urging the bishops and archbishops to further his plans. He did not meet with much success, however, although the Dominicans and the Friars Minor did their best to help him. Still some cities like Milan, Verona, Piacenza and Vercelli adopted the measures of persecution which he proposed. At Milan, Peter of Verona, a Dominican, on September 15, 1233, had the laws of the Pope and the Senator of Rome inscribed in the city's statutes. The *animadversio debita* was henceforth interpreted to mean the penalty of the stake. "In this year," writes a chronicler of the time, "the people of Milan began to burn heretics." In the month of July, sixty heretics were sent to the stake at Verona. The podestà of Piacenza sent to the Pope the heretics he had arrested. Vercelli, at the instance of the Franciscan, Henry of Milan, incorporated in 1233 into its statutes the law of the Senator of Rome and the imperial law of 1224; it, however, omitted in the last named law the clause which decreed the penalty of cutting out the tongue. In Germany, the Dominican, Conrad of Marburg, was particularly active, in virtue of his commission from Gregory IX. In accordance with the imperial law, we find him sentencing to the stake a great number of heretics.

It may be admitted, however, that in his excessive zeal he even went beyond the desires of the sovereign pontiff. Gregory IX did not find everywhere so marked an eagerness to carry out his wishes. A number of the cities of Italy for a long time continued to punish obstinate heretics according to the penal code of Innocent III, *i. e.*, by banishment and confiscation.

That the penalty of the stake was used at this time in France is proved by the burning of one hundred and eighty-three Bulgarians or Bugres at Mont-Wimer in 1239, and by two important documents, the *Établissements de Saint Louis* and the *Coutumes de Beauvaisis*.

" As soon as the ecclesiastical judge has discovered, after due examination, that the suspect is a heretic, he must hand him over to the secular arm; and the secular judge must send him to the stake." [1] Beaumanoir says the same thing: " In such a case, the secular court must aid the Church; for when the Church condemns any one as a heretic, she is obliged to hand him over to the secular arm to be sent to the stake; for she herself cannot put any one to death." [2]

It is a question whether this legislation is merely the codification of the custom introduced by popular up-

---

[1] *Établissements de Saint Louis*, ch. cxxiii.
[2] *Coutumes de Beauvaisis*, xi, 2; cf. xxx, 11, ed. Beugnot, vol. i, pp. 157, 413.

risings against heresy and by certain royal decrees, or whether it owes its origin to the law of Frederic II which Gregory IX tried to enforce in France, as he had done in Germany and Italy. This second hypothesis is hardly probable. The tribunals of the Inquisition did not have to import into France the penalty of the stake; they found it already established in both central and northern France.

In fact, Gregory IX urged everywhere the enforcement of the existing laws against heresy, and where none existed he introduced a very severe system of prosecution. He was the first, moreover, to establish an extraordinary and permanent tribunal for heresy trials—an institution which afterwards became known as the monastic Inquisition.

. . . .

The prosecution and the punishment of heretics in every diocese was one of the chief duties of the bishops, the natural defenders of orthodoxy. While heresy appeared at occasional intervals, they had little or no difficulty in fulfilling their duty. But when the Cathari and the Patarins had sprung up everywhere, especially in southern Italy and France and northern Spain, the secrecy of their movements made the task of the bishops extremely hard and complicated. Rome soon perceived that they were not very zealous in prosecuting heresy. To put an end to this neglect, Lucius III, jointly with the Emperor Frederic Barbarossa and the bishops of his court, enacted a decretal at Verona in 1184, regulating the *episcopal inquisition*.

All bishops and archbishops were commanded to visit personally once or twice a year, or to empower their archdeacons or other clerics to visit, every parish in which heresy was thought to exist. They were to compel two or three trustworthy men, or, if need be, all the inhabitants of the city, to swear that they would denounce every suspect who attended secret assemblies, or whose manner of living differed from that of the ordinary Catholic. After the bishop had questioned all who had been brought before his tribunal, he was empowered to punish them as he deemed fit, unless the accused succeeded in establishing their innocence. All who superstitiously refused to take the required oath (we have seen how the Cathari considered it criminal to take an oath) were to be condemned and punished as heretics, and if they refused to abjure they were handed over to the secular arm.[1] This was an attempt to recall the bishops to a sense of their duty. The Lateran Council of 1215 re-enacted the laws of Lucius III; and to ensure their enforcement it decreed that every bishop who neglected his duty should be deposed, and another consecrated in his place.[2] The Council of Narbonne in 1227 likewise ordered the bishops to appoint synodal witnesses (*testes synodales*) in every parish to prosecute heretics.[3] But all these decrees, although properly countersigned and placed in the archives, remained practically a dead letter. In the first place it was very difficult to obtain the synodal witnesses. And again, as a contemporary bishop, Lucas de Tuy, assures us, the bishops for the most part were not at all anxious to prosecute heresy. When reproached for their inaction they replied:

---

[1] Lucius III, *Ep.* clxxi, Migne, P. L., vol. cci, col. 1297 and seq.
[2] The Bull *Excommunicamus*, Decretals, cap. xiii, in fine, *De hæreticis*, lib. v, tit. vii.
[3] Can. 14, Labbe, *Concilia*, vol. xi, pars i, col. 307, 308.

THE INQUISITION

" How can we condemn those who are neither convicted nor confessed? "[1]

The Popes, as the rulers of Christendom, tried to make up for the indifference of the bishops by sending their legates to hunt for the Cathari in their most hidden retreats. But they soon realized that this legatine inquisition was ineffective.[2]

" Bishop and legate," writes Lea, " were alike unequal to the task of discovering those who carefully shrouded themselves under the cloak of the most orthodox observance; and when by chance a nest of heretics was brought to light, the learning and skill of the average Ordinary failed to elicit a confession from those who professed the most entire accord with the teachings of Rome. In the absence of overt acts, it was difficult to reach the secret thoughts of the sectary. Trained experts were needed whose sole business it should be to unearth the offenders, and extort a confession of their guilt."

At an opportune moment, therefore, two mendicant orders, the Dominicans and the Franciscans, were instituted to meet the new needs of the Church. Both orders devoted themselves to preaching; the Dominicans were especially learned in the ecclesiastical sciences, *i. e.*, canon law and theology.

" The establishment of these orders," continues Lea, " seemed a providential interposition to supply the Church of Christ with what it most sorely needed.

---

[1] Lucas Tudensis, *De altera vita fideique controversiis adversus Albigensium errores*, cap. xix, in the *Bibliotheca Patrum*, 4 ed. vol. iv, col. 575–714. Lucas was Bishop of Tuy in Galicia, from 1239 to 1249.

[2] Cf. Lea, *op. cit.*, vol. i, p. 315 and seq.

As the necessity grew apparent of special and permanent tribunals, devoted exclusively to the widespread sin of heresy, there was every reason why they should be wholly free from the local jealousies and enmities which might tend to the prejudice of the innocent, or the local favoritism which might connive at the escape of the guilty. If, in addition to this freedom from local partialities, the examiners and judges were men specially trained to the detection and conversion of the heretics; if also, they had by irrevocable vows renounced the world; if they could acquire no wealth, and were dead to the enticement of pleasure, every guarantee seemed to be afforded that their momentous duties would be fulfilled with the strictest justice—that while the purity of the faith would be protected, there would be no unnecessary oppression or cruelty or persecution dictated by private interests and personal revenge. Their unlimited popularity was also a warrant that they would receive far more efficient assistance in their arduous labors than could be expected by the bishops, whose position was generally that of antagonism to their flocks, and to the petty seigneurs and powerful barons whose aid was indispensable.[1]

Gregory IX fully understood the help that the Dominicans and Franciscans could render him as agents of the Inquisition throughout Christendom.

It is probable that the Senator of Rome refers to them in his oath in 1231, when he speaks of the *Inquisitores datos ab Ecclesia*.[2] Frederic II, in his law of 1232, also mentions the *Inquisitores ab apostolica*

[1] Lea, *op. cit.*, pp. 318, 319.
[2] Raynaldi, *Annales*, ad ann. 1231, sect. 16, 17.

sede datos.[1] The Dominican Albéric traveled through Lombardy in November, 1232, with the title of *Inquisitor hæreticæ pravitatis*.[2] In 1231 a similar commission was entrusted to the Dominicans of Freisach and to the famous Conrad of Marburg. Finally, to quote but one more instance, Gregory IX, in 1233, wrote an eloquent letter to the bishops of southern France in which he said: " We, seeing you engrossed in the whirlwind of cares, and scarce able to breathe in the pressure of overwhelming anxieties, think it well to divide your burdens, that they may be more easily borne. We have therefore determined to send preaching friars against the heretics of France and the adjoining provinces, and we beg, warn, and exhort you, ordering you, as you reverence the Holy See, to receive them kindly, and to treat them well, giving them in this as in all else, favor, counsel, and aid, that they may fulfill their office."

Their duties are outlined in a letter of Gregory IX to Conrad of Marburg, October 11, 1231: " When you arrive in a city, summon the bishops, clergy and people, and preach a solemn sermon on faith; then select certain men of good repute to help you in trying the heretics and suspects denounced before your tribunal. All who on examination are found guilty or suspected of heresy must promise to absolutely obey the commands of the Church; if they refuse, you must prosecute them, according to the statutes which we have recently promulgated." We have in these instructions all the procedure of the Inquisition· the time of grace; the call for witnesses and their testi-

[1] Cap. iii, in the *Mon. Germ.*, *Leges*, sect. iv, vol. ii, p. 196.
[2] Potthast, *Regesta Roman. Pontif.*, no. 904, 1.

mony; the interrogation of the accused; the reconciliation of repentant heretics; the condemnation of obdurate heretics.

Each detail of this procedure calls for a few words of explanation.

The Inquisitor first summoned every heretic of the city to appear before him within a certain fixed time, which as a rule did not exceed thirty days. This period was called "the time of grace" (*tempus gratiæ*). The heretics who abjured during this period were treated with leniency. If secret heretics, they were dismissed with only a slight secret penance; if public heretics, they were exempted from the penalties of death and life imprisonment, and sentenced either to make a short pilgrimage, or to undergo one of the ordinary canonical penances.

If the heretics failed to come forward of their own accord, they were to be denounced by the Catholic people. At first the number of witnesses required to make an accusation valid was not determined; later on two were declared necessary. In the beginning, the Inquisition could only accept the testimony of men and women of good repute; and the Church for a long time maintained that no one should be admitted as an accuser who was a heretic, was excommunicated, a homicide, a thief, a sorcerer, a diviner, or the bearer of false witness. But her hatred of heresy led her later on to set aside this law, when the faith was in question. As early as the twelfth century, Gratian had declared that the testimony of infamous and heretical witnesses might be accepted in trials for heresy.[1]

[1] Pars ii, *Causa* ii, quaest. vii, cap. xxii; *Causa vi*, quaest. i, cap. xix.

The edicts of Frederic II declared that heretics could not testify in the courts, but this disability was removed when they were called upon to testify against other suspects.[1] In the beginning, the Inquisitors were loath to accept such testimony. But in 1261 Alexander IV assured them that it was lawful to do so.[2] Henceforth the testimony of a heretic was considered valid, although it was always left to the discretion of the Inquisition to reject it at will. This principle was finally incorporated into the canon law, and was enforced by constant practice. All legal exceptions were henceforth declared inoperative except that of moral enmity.[3]

Witnesses for the defence rarely presented themselves. Very seldom do we come across any mention of them. This is readily understood, for they would almost inevitably have been suspected as accomplices and abettors of heresy. For the same reason, the accused were practically denied the help of counsel. Innocent III had forbidden advocates and scriveners to lend aid or counsel to heretics and their abettors.[4] This prohibition, which in the mind of the Pope was intended only for defiant and acknowledged heretics, was gradually extended to every suspect who was striving to prove his innocence.[5]

[1] *Historia diplomatica Frederici II*, vol. iv, pp. 299, 300.

[2] Bull *Consuluit*, of January 23, 1261, in Eymeric, *Directorium inquisitorum*, Appendix, p. 40.

[3] Eymeric, *ibid.*, 3ª pars, quaest. lxvii, pp. 606, 607. Pegna, *ibid.*, pp. 607, 609, declares that great cruelty or even insulting words—*v. g.*, to call a man *cornutus* or a woman *meretrix*—might come under the head of enmity, and invalidate a man's testimony.

[4] Decretals, cap. xi, *De hæreticis*, lib. v, tit. vii.

[5] Eymeric, *Directorium inquisitorum*, 3ª pars, quaest. xxxix, p. 565; cf. 446. Sometimes, however, the accused was granted

Heretics or suspects, therefore, denounced to the Inquisition generally found themselves without counsel before their judges.

They personally had to answer the various charges of the indictment (*capitula*) made against them. It certainly would have been a great help to them, to have known the names of their accusers. But the fear—well-founded it was true[1]—that the accused or their friends would revenge themselves on their accusers, induced the Inquisitors to withhold the names of the witnesses.[2] The only way in which the prisoner could invalidate the testimony against him was to name all his mortal enemies. If his accusers happened to be among them, their testimony was thrown out of court.[3] But otherwise, he was obliged to prove the falsity of the accusation against him—

counsel, but *juxta juris formam ac stylum et usum officii Inquisitionis;* cf. Vidal, *Le tribunal d'Inquisition*, in the *Annales de Saint Louis des Français*, vol. ix (1905), p. 299, note. Eymeric himself grants one (*Directorium*, pp. 451–453). But this lawyer was merely to persuade his client to confess his heresy; he was rather the lawyer of the court than of the accused. Vidal, *op. cit.*, pp. 302, 303. Pegna, however, says (in Eymeric *Directorium*, 2ᵃ pars, ch. xi, Comm. 10) that in his time the accused was allowed counsel, if he were only suspected of heresy. Cf. Tanon, *op. cit.*, pp. 400, 401.

[1] Guillem Pelhisse tells us that the Cathari sometimes killed those who had denounced their brethren. *Chronique*, ed. Douai, p. 90. A certain Arnold Dominici, who had denounced seven heretics, was killed at night in his bed by "the Believers." *Ibid.*, pp. 98, 99.

[2] Eymeric, *Directorium*, 3ᵃ pars, q. 72. The law on this point varied from time to time. When Boniface VIII incorporated into the canon law the rule of withholding the names of witnesses, he expressly said that they might be produced, if there was no danger in doing so. Cap. 20, Sexto v, 2.

[3] Eymeric, *Directorium*, 3ᵃ pars, *De defensionibus reorum*, p. 446 and seq.

a practically impossible undertaking. For if two witnesses, considered of good repute by the Inquisitor, agreed in accusing the prisoner, his fate was at once settled; whether he confessed or not, he was declared a heretic.

After the prisoner had been found guilty, he could choose one of two things; he could abjure his heresy and manifest his repentance by accepting the penance imposed by his judge, or he could obstinately persist either in his denial or profession of heresy, accepting resolutely all the consequences of such an attitude.

If the heretic abjured he knelt before the Inquisitor as a penitent before his confessor. He had no reason to fear his judge. For, properly speaking, he did not inflict punishment.

" The mission of the Inquisition," writes Lea, " was to save men's souls; to recall them to the way of salvation, and to assign salutary penance to those who sought it, like a father-confessor with his penitent. Its sentences, therefore, were not like those of an earthly judge, the retaliation of society on the wrong-doer, or deterrent examples to prevent the spread of crime; they were simply imposed for the benefit of the erring soul, to wash away its sin. The Inquisitors themselves habitually speak of their ministrations in this sense." [1]

But " the sin of heresy was too grave to be expiated simply by contrition and amendment." [2] The Inquisitor, therefore, pointed out other means of expiation: "The penances customarily imposed by the Inquisition were comparatively few in number. They

[1] Lea, *op. cit.*, p. 459.
[2] Lea, *ibid.*, p. 463.

consisted, firstly, of pious observances—recitation of prayers, frequenting of churches, the discipline, fasting, pilgrimages, and fines nominally for pious uses,—such as a confessor might impose on his ordinary penitents." These were for offences of trifling import. " Next in grade are the *pœnæ confusibiles*,—the humiliating and degrading penances, of which the most important was the wearing of yellow crosses sewed upon the garments; and, finally, the severest punishment among those strictly within the competence of the Holy Office, the *murus* or prison." [1]

If the heretic refused to abjure, his obduracy put an end to the judge's leniency, and withdrew him at once from his jurisdiction.

" The Inquisitor never condemned to death, but merely withdrew the protection of the Church from the hardened and impenitent sinner who afforded no hope of conversion, or from him who showed by relapse that there was no trust to be placed in his pretended repentance." [2]

It was at this juncture that the State intervened. The ecclesiastical judge handed over the heretic to the secular arm, which simply enforced the legal penalty of the stake. However, the law allowed the heretic to abjure even at the foot of the stake; in that case his sentence was commuted to life imprisonment.

It is hard to conceive of a greater responsibility than that of a mediæval Inquisitor. The life or death of the heretic was practically at his disposal. The Church, therefore, required him to possess in a preeminent degree the qualities of an impartial judge.

[1] Lea, *ibid.*, p. 462.
[2] Lea, *ibid.*, p. 460.

Bernard Gui, the most experienced Inquisitor of his time (1308–1323), thus paints for us the portrait of the ideal Inquisitor: " He should be diligent and fervent in his zeal for religious truth, for the salvation of souls, and for the destruction of heresy. He should always be calm in times of trial and difficulty, and never give way to outbursts of anger or temper. He should be a brave man, ready to face death if necessary, but while never cowardly running from danger, he should never be foolhardy rushing into it. He should be unmoved by the entreaties or the bribes of those who appear before his tribunal; still he must not harden his heart to the point of refusing to delay or mitigate punishment, as circumstances may require from time to time.

" In doubtful cases, he should be very careful not to believe too easily what may appear probable, and yet in reality is false; nor, on the other hand, should he stubbornly refuse to believe what may appear improbable, and yet is frequently true. He should zealously discuss and examine every case, so as to be sure to make a just decision. . . . Let the love of truth and mercy, the special qualities of every good judge, shine in his countenance, and let his sentences never be prompted by avarice or cruelty." [1]

This portrait corresponds to the idea that Gregory IX had of the true Inquisitor. In the instructions which he gave to the terrible Conrad of Marburg, October 21, 1223, he took good care to warn him to be prudent as well as zealous: " Punish if you will," he said, " the wicked and perverse, but see that no innocent person suffers at your hands:" *ut puniatur sic*

[1] *Practica Inquisitionis*, pars 6ᵃ, ed. Douais, 1886, pp. 231–233.

temeritas perversorum, quod innocentiæ puritas non lædatur. Gregory IX cannot be accused of injustice, but he will ever be remembered as the Pope who established the Inquisition as a permanent tribunal, and did his utmost to enforce everywhere the death penalty for heresy.

This Pope was, in certain respects, a very slave to the letter of the law. The protests of St. Augustine and many other early Fathers did not affect him in the least. In the beginning, while he was legate, he merely insisted upon the enforcement of the penal code of Innocent III, which did not decree any punishment severer than banishment, but he soon began to regard heresy as a crime similar to treason, and therefore subject to the same penalty, death. Certain ecclesiastics of his court with extremely logical minds, and rulers like Pedro II of Aragon and Frederic II, had reached the same conclusion, even before he did. Finally, in the fourth year of his pontificate, and undoubtedly after mature deliberation, he decided to compel the princes and the podestà to enforce the law condemning heretics to the stake.

He did his utmost to bring this about. He did not forget, however, that the Church could not concern herself in sentences of death. In fact, his law of 1231 decrees that: " Heretics condemned by the Church are to be handed over to the secular courts to receive due punishment (*animadversio debita*)." [1] The emperor Frederic II had the same notion of the distinction between the two powers. His law of 1224 points out carefully that heretics convicted by an ecclesiastical trial are to be burned in the name of the civil authority:

[1] *Decretales*, cap. xv, *De Hæreticis*, lib. v, tit. vii.

auctoritate nostra ignis judicio concremandus.¹ The imperial law of 1232 likewise declares that heretics condemned by the Church are to be brought before a secular tribunal to receive the punishment they deserve.² This explains why Gregory IX did not believe that in handing over heretics to the secular arm he participated directly or indirectly in a death sentence.³ The tribunals of the Inquisition which he established in no way modified this concept of ecclesiastical justice. The Papacy, the guardian of orthodoxy for the universal Church, simply found that the Dominicans and the Franciscans were more docile instruments than the episcopate for the suppression of heresy. But whether the Inquisition was under the direction of the bishops or the monks, it could have been conducted on the same lines.

But, as a matter of fact, it unfortunately changed

---

¹ *Mon. Germ., Leges*, sect. iv, vol. ii, p. 126.
² *Ibid.*, p. 196.
³ Lea writes (*op. cit.*, vol. i, p. 536, note): "Gregory IX had no scruple in asserting the duty of the Church to shed the blood of heretics." In a brief of 1234 to the Archbishop of Sens, he says: *Nec enim decuit Apostolicam Sedem, in oculis suis cum Madianita cœunte Judæo, manum suam a sanguine prohibere, ne si secus ageret non custodire populum Israel . . . videretur.* Ripoll, i, 66. This is certainly a serious charge, but the citation he gives implies something altogether different. Lea has been deceived himself, and in turn has misled his readers, by a comparison which he mistook for a doctrinal document. The context, we think, clearly shows that the Pope was making a comparison between the Holy See and the Jewish leader Phinees, who had slain an Israelite and a harlot of Madian, in the very act of their crime (Num. xxv. 6, 7). That does not imply that the Church uses the same weapons. Even if the comparison is not a very happy one, still we must not exaggerate its import. The Pope's letter did not even mention the execution of heretics. Ripoll, *Bullarium ord. FF. Prædicatorum*, vol. i, p. 66.

completely under the direction of the monks. The
change effected by them in the ecclesiastical procedure
resulted wholly to the detriment of the accused. The
safeguards for their defense were in part done away
with. A pretense was made to satisfy the demands of
justice by requiring that the Inquisitors be prudent
and impartial judges. But this made everything depend upon individuals, whereas the law itself should
have been just and impartial. In this respect, the
criminal procedure of the Inquisition is markedly
inferior to the criminal procedure of the Middle Ages.

CHAPTER VII

SIXTH PERIOD

DEVELOPMENT OF THE INQUISITION

INNOCENT IV AND THE USE OF TORTURE

THE successors of Gregory IX were not long in perceiving certain defects in the system of the Inquisition. They tried their best to remedy them, although their efforts were not always directed with the view of mitigating its rigor. We will indicate briefly their various decrees pertaining to the tribunals, the penalties and the procedure of the Inquisition.

In appointing the Dominicans and the Franciscans to suppress heresy, Gregory IX did not dream of abolishing the episcopal Inquisition. This was still occasionally carried on with its rival, whose procedure it finally adopted. Indeed no tribunal of the Inquisition could operate in a diocese without the permission of the Bishop, whom it was supposed to aid. But it was inevitable that the Inquisitors would in time encroach upon the episcopal authority, and relying upon their papal commission proceed to act as independent judges. This abuse frequently attracted the attention of the Popes, who, after some hesitation, finally settled the law on this point.

THE INQUISITION

"If previous orders requiring it" (episcopal concurrence), writes Lea, "had not been treated with contempt, Innocent IV would not have been obliged, in 1254, to reiterate the instructions that no condemnations to death or life imprisonment should be uttered without consulting the Bishops; and in 1255 he enjoined Bishop and Inquisitor to interpret in consultation any obscurities in the laws against heresy, and to administer the lighter penalties of deprivation of office and preferment. This recognition of episcopal jurisdiction was annulled by Alexander IV, who, after some vacillation, in 1257 rendered the Inquisition independent by releasing it from the necessity of consulting with the Bishops even in cases of obstinate and confessed heretics, and this he repeated in 1260. Then there was a reaction. In 1262, Urban IV, in an elaborate code of instructions, formally revived the consultation in all cases involving the death penalty or perpetual imprisonment; and this was repeated by Clement IV in 1265. Either these instructions, however, were revoked in some subsequent enactment, or they soon fell into desuetude, for in 1273, Gregory X, after alluding to the action of Alexander IV in annulling consultation, proceeds to direct that Inquisitors in deciding upon sentences shall proceed in accordance with the counsel of the Bishops or their delegates, so that the episcopal authority might share in decisions of such moment."[1]

This decretal remained henceforth the law. But as the Inquisitors at times seemed to act as if it did not exist, Boniface VIII and Clement IV strengthened it by declaring null and void all grave sentences in which

[1] Lea, *op. cit.*, p. 335.

THE INQUISITION 99

the Bishop had not been consulted.¹ The consultation, however, between the Bishop and Inquisitor could be conducted through delegates. In insisting upon this, the Popes proved that they were anxious to give the sentences of the Inquisition every possible guarantee of perfect justice.

Another way in which the Popes labored to render the sentences of the Inquisition just, was the institution of experts. As the questions which arose before the tribunals in matters of heresy were often very complex, " it was soon found requisite to associate with the Inquisitors in the rendering of sentences men versed in the civil and canon law, which had by this time become an intricate study, requiring the devotion of a lifetime. Accordingly they were empowered to call in experts to deliberate with them over the evidence. and advise with them on the sentence to be rendered.' ²

The official records of the sentences of the Inquisition frequently mention the presence of these experts, *periti* and *boni viri*. Their number, which varied according to circumstances, was generally large. At a consultation called by the Inquisitors in January, 1329, at the Bishop's palace in Pamiers, there were thirty-five present, nine of whom were jurisconsults; and at another in September, 1329, there were fifty-one present, twenty of whom were civil lawyers.

" At a comparatively early date, the practice was adopted of allowing a number of culprits to accumulate, whose fate was determined and announced in a solemn *Sermo* or *auto-da-fé*. . . . In the final shape

¹ *Sexto*, lib. v, tit. ii, cap. 17, *Per hoc;* Clementin· lib **v. tit.** iii, cap. i, *Multorum querela*.
² Lea, *op. cit.*, vol. i, p. 388.

which the assembly of counsellors assumed, we find it summoned to meet on Fridays, the *Sermo* always taking place on Sundays. When the number of criminals was large, there was not much time for deliberation in special cases. The assessors were always to be jurists and Mendicant Friars, selected by the Inquisitor in such numbers as he saw fit. They were severally sworn on the Gospels to secrecy, and to give good and wise counsel, each one according to his conscience, and to the knowledge vouchsafed him by God. The Inquisitor then read over his summary of each case, sometimes withholding the name of the accused, and they voted the sentence, " Penance at the discretion of the Inquisitor "—" that person is to be imprisoned, or abandoned to the secular arm "—while the Gospels lay on the table " so that our judgment might come from the face of God, and our eyes might see justice." [1]

We have here the beginnings of our modern jury. As a rule, the Inquisitors followed the advice of their counsellors, save when they themselves favored a less severe sentence. The labor of these experts was considerable, and often lasted several days. "A brief summary of each case was submitted to them. Eymeric maintained that the whole case ought to be submitted to them; and that was undoubtedly the common practice. But Pegna, on the other hand, thought it was better to withhold from the assessors the names of both the witnesses and the prisoners. He declares that this was the common practice of the Inquisition, at least as far as the names were concerned. This was also the practice of the Inquisitors of southern

[1] Lea, *op. cit.*, vol. i, p. 389.

France, as Bernard Gui tells us. The majority of the counsellors received a brief summary of the case, the names being withheld. Only a very few of them were deemed worthy to read the full text of all the interrogatories."[1]

We can readily see how the *periti* or *boni viri*, who were called upon to decide the guilt or innocence of the accused from evidence considered in the abstract, without any knowledge of the prisoners' names or motives, could easily make mistakes. In fact, they did not have data enough to enable them to decide a concrete case. For tribunals are to judge criminals and not crimes, just as physicians treat sick people and not diseases in the abstract. We know that the same disease calls for a different treatment in different individuals; in like manner a crime must be judged with due reference to the mentality of the one who has committed it. The Inquisition did not seem to understand this.[2]

The assembly of experts, therefore, instituted by the Popes did not obtain the good results that were expected. But we must, at least, in justice admit that the Popes did their utmost to protect the tribunals of the Inquisition from the arbitrary action of individual judges, by requiring the Inquisitors to consult both the *boni viri* and the Bishops.

Over the various penalties of the Inquisition, the

[1] Tanon, *op. cit.*, p. 421.
[2] Even in our day the jury is bound to decide on the merits of the case submitted to it, without regarding the consequences of its verdict. The foreman reminds the jurymen in advance that " they will be false to their oath if, in giving their decision, they are biased by the consideration of the punishment their verdict will entail upon the prisoner."

Popes likewise exercised a supervision which was always just and at times most kindly.

The greatest penalties which the Inquisition could inflict were life imprisonment, and abandonment of the prisoner to the secular arm. It is only with regard to the first of these penalties that we see the clemency of both Popes and Councils. Any one who considers the rough manners of this period, must admit that the Church did a great deal to mitigate the excessive cruelty of the mediæval prisons.

The Council of Toulouse, in 1229, decreed that repentant heretics " must be imprisoned, in such a way that they could not corrupt others." It also declared that the Bishop was to provide for the prisoners' needs out of their confiscated property. Such measures betoken an earnest desire to safeguard the health, and to a certain degree the liberty of the prisoners. In fact, the documents we possess prove that the condemned sometimes enjoyed a great deal of freedom, and were allowed to receive from their friends an additional supply of food, even when the prison fare was ample.

But in many places the prisoners, even before their trial, were treated with great cruelty. " The papal orders were that they (the prisons) should be constructed of small, dark cells for solitary confinement, only taking care that the *enormis rigor* of the incarceration should not extinguish life." [1] But this last provision was not always carried out. Too often the prisoners were confined in narrow cells full of disease, and totally unfit for human habitation. The Popes, learning this sad state of affairs, tried to remedy it.

[1] Lea, *op. cit.*, vol. i, p. 491.

THE INQUISITION 103

Clement V was particularly zealous in his attempts at prison reform.[1] That he succeeded in bettering, at least for a time, the lot of these unfortunates, in whom he interested himself, cannot be denied.[2]

If the reforms he decreed were not all carried out, the blame must be laid to the door of those appointed to enforce them. History frees him from all responsibility.

The part played by the Popes, the Councils, and the Inquisitors in the infliction of the death penalty does not appear in so favorable a light. While not directly participating in the death sentences, they were still very eager for the execution of the heretics they abandoned to the secular arm. This is well attested by both documents and facts.

Lucius III, at the Council of Verona in 1184, ordered sovereigns to swear, in the presence of their Bishops, to execute fully and conscientiously the ecclesiastical and civil laws against heresy. If they refused or neglected to do this, they themselves were liable to excommunication and their rebellious cities to interdict.[3]

---

[1] He ordered that the prisons be kept in good condition, that they be looked after by both Bishop and Inquisitor, each of whom was to appoint a jailer who would keep the prison keys, that all provisions sent to the prisoners should be faithfully given them, etc. Cf. Decretal *Multorum querela* in Eymeric, *Directorium*, p. 112.

[2] His legates Pierre de la Chapelle and Béranger de Frédol visited in April, 1306, the prisons of Carcassonne and Albi, changed the jailers, removed the irons from the prisoners, and made others leave the subterraneous cells in which they had been confined. Douais, *Documents*, vol. ii, p. 304 seq. Cf. Compayré, *Études historiques sur l'Albigeois*, pp. 240–245.

[3] Decretal *Ad abolendam*, in the Decretals, cap, ix, *de Hæreticis*, lib. v, tit. vii. Cf. Sexto, lib. v, tit. ii, c. 2. *Ut Officium;* Council of Arles, 1254, can. iii; Council of Béziers, 1246, can. ix.

Innocent IV, in 1252, enacted a law still more severe, insisting on the infliction of the death penalty upon heretics. "When," he says, "heretics condemned by the Bishop, his Vicar, or the Inquisitors, have been abandoned to the secular arm, the podestà or ruler of the city must take charge of them at once, and within five days enforce the laws against them."[1]

This law, or rather the bull *Ad Extirpanda*, which contains it, was to be inscribed in perpetuity in all the local statute books. Any attempt to modify it was a crime, which condemned the offender to perpetual infamy, and a fine enforced by the ban. Moreover, each podestà, at the beginning and end of his term, was required to have this bull read in all places designated by the Bishop and the Inquisitors, and to erase from the statute books all laws to the contrary.

At the same time, Innocent IV issued instructions to the Inquisitors of upper Italy, urging them to have this bull and the edicts of Frederic II inserted in the statutes of the various cities.[2] And to prevent mistakes being made as to which imperial edicts he wished enforced, he repeated these instructions in 1254, and inserted in one of his bulls the cruel laws of Frederic II, viz., the edict of Ravenna, *Commissis nobis*, which decreed the death of obdurate heretics; and the Sicilian law, *Inconsutilem tunicam*, which expressly decreed that such heretics be sent to the stake.

These decrees remained the law as long as the Inquisition lasted. The bull *Ad Extirpanda* was, however, slightly modified from time to time. "In 1265,

[1] Eymeric, *Directorium*, Appendix, p. 8.
[2] Cf. the bulls *Cum adversus*, *Tunc potissime*, *Ex Commissis nobis*, etc., in Eymeric, *ibid.*, pp. 9–12.

Clement IV again went over it, carefully making some changes, principally in adding the word ' Inquisitors ' in passages where Innocent had only designated the Bishops and Friars, thus showing that the Inquisition had, during the interval, established itself as the recognized instrumentality in the prosecution of heresy, and the next year he repeated Innocent's emphatic order to the Inquisitors to enforce the insertion of his legislation and that of his predecessors upon the statute books everywhere, with the free use of excommunication and interdict." [1]

A little later, Nicholas IV, who during his short pontificate (1288-1292), greatly favored the Inquisition in its work, re-enacted the bulls of Innocent IV and Clement IV, and ordered the enforcement of the laws of Frederic II, lest, perchance, they might fall into desuetude.[2]

It is therefore proved beyond question that the Church, in the person of the Popes, used every means at her disposal, especially excommunication, to compel the State to enforce the infliction of the death penalty upon heretics. This excommunication, moreover, was all the more dreaded, because, according to the canons, the one excommunicated, unless absolved from the censure, was regarded as a heretic himself within a year's time, and was liable therefore to the death penalty.[3] The princes of the day, therefore, had no

---

[1] Lea, *op. cit.*, vol. i, p. 339.

[2] *Registers*, published by Langlois, no. 4253.

[3] Alexander IV decreed this penalty against the contumacious. Sexto, *De Hæreticis*, cap. vii. Boniface VIII extended it to those princes and magistrates who did not enforce the sentences of the Inquisition. Sexto, *De Hæreticis*, cap. xviii in Eymeric, 2ª pars, p. 110.

other way of escaping this penalty, except by faithfully carrying out the sentence of the Church.

. . . .

The Church is also responsible for having introduced torture into the proceedings of the Inquisition. This cruel practice was introduced by Innocent IV in 1252.

Torture had left too terrible an impression upon the minds of the early Christians to permit of their employing it in their own tribunals. The barbarians who founded the commonwealths of Europe, with the exception of the Visigoths, knew nothing of this brutal method of extorting confessions. The only thing of the kind which they allowed was flogging, which, according to St. Augustine, was rather akin to the correction of children by their parents. Gratian, who recommends it in his *Decretum*,[1] lays it down as an "accepted rule of canon law that no confession is to be extorted by torture."[2] Besides, Nicholas I, in his instructions to the Bulgarians, had formally denounced the torturing of prisoners.[3] He advised that the testimony of three persons be required for conviction; if these could not be obtained, the prisoner's oath upon the Gospels was to be considered sufficient.

The ecclesiastical tribunals borrowed from Germany another method of proving crime, viz., the ordeals, or judgments of God.

There was the duel, the ordeal of the cross, the ordeal of boiling water, the ordeal of fire, and the ordeal of cold water. They had a great vogue in

---

[1] *Causa* v, quæst. v, Illi qui, cap. iv.
[2] *Causa* xv, quæst. vi, cap. i.
[3] *Responsa ad Consulta Bulgarorum*, cap. lxxxvi, Labbe, *Concilia*, vol. viii, col. 544.

nearly all the Latin countries, especially in Germany and France. But about the twelfth century they deservedly fell into great disfavor, until at last the Popes, particularly Innocent III, Honorius III, and Gregory IX, legislated them out of existence.[1]

At the very moment the Popes were condemning the ordeals, the revival of the Roman law throughout the West was introducing the customs of antiquity. It was then "that jurists began to feel the need of torture, and accustom themselves to the idea of its introduction. The earliest instances with which I have met," writes Lea, "occur in the Veronese code of 1228, and the Sicilian constitutions of Frederic II in 1231, and in both of these the references to it show how sparingly and hesitatingly it was employed. Even Frederic, in his ruthless edicts, from 1220 to 1239, makes no allusion to it, but in accordance with the Verona decree of Lucius III, prescribes the recognized form of canonical purgation for the trial of all suspected heretics."[2]

The use of torture, as Tanon has pointed out, had perhaps never been altogether discontinued. Some ecclesiastical tribunals, at least in Paris, made use of it in extremely grave cases, at the close of the twelfth and beginning of the thirteenth centuries.[3] But this was exceptional: in Italy, apparently, it had never been used.

Gregory IX ignored all references to torture made in the Veronese code, and the constitutions of Frederic

[1] Decretals, lib. v, tit. xxxv, cap. i–iii. Cf. Vacandard, *L'Église et les Ordalies* in *Études de critique et d'histoire*, 3d ed., Paris, 1906, pp. 191–215.

[2] Lea, *op. cit.*, vol. i, p. 421.

[3] Tanon, *op. cit.*, pp. 362–373.

II. But Innocent IV, feeling undoubtedly that it was a quick and effective method for detecting criminals, authorized the tribunals of the Inquisition to employ it. In his bull *Ad Extirpanda*, he says: " The podestà or ruler (of the city) is hereby ordered to force all captured heretics to confess and accuse their accomplices by torture which will not imperil life or injure limb, just as thieves and robbers are forced to accuse their accomplices, and to confess their crimes; for these heretics are true thieves, murderers of souls, and robbers of the sacraments of God."[1] The Pope here tries to defend the use of torture, by classing heretics with thieves and murderers. A mere comparison is his only argument.

This law of Innocent IV was renewed and confirmed November 30, 1259, by Alexander IV,[2] and again on November 3, 1265, by Clement IV.[3] The restriction of Innocent III to use torture "which should not imperil life or injure limb" (*Cogere citra membri diminutionem et mortis periculum*), left a great deal to the discretion of the Inquisitors. Besides flogging, the other punishments inflicted upon those who refused to confess the crime of which they were accused were antecedent imprisonment, the rack, the *strappado*, and the burning coals.

When after the first interrogatory the prisoner denied what the Inquisitors believed to be very probable or certain, he was thrown into prison. The *durus carcer et arcta vita* was deemed an excellent method of extorting confessions.

---

[1] Bull *Ad Extirpanda*, in Eymeric, *Directorium*, Appendix, p. 8.
[2] Potthast, *Regesta*, no. 17714.
[3] *Ibid.*, no. 19433.

"It was pointed out," says Lea, "that judicious restriction of diet not only reduced the body, but weakened the will, and rendered the prisoner less able to resist alternate threats of death and promises of mercy. Starvation, in fact, was reckoned one of the regular and most efficient methods to subdue unwilling witnesses and defendants."[1] This was the usual method employed in Languedoc. "It is the only method," writes Mgr. Douais,[2] "to extort confessions mentioned either in the records of the notary of the Inquisition of Carcassonne[3] or in the sentences of Bernard Gui. It was also the practice of the Inquisitors across the Rhine."

Still the use of torture, especially of the rack and the *strappado*, was not unknown in southern Europe, even before the promulgation of Innocent's bull *Ad Extirpanda*.

The rack was a triangular frame, on which the prisoner was stretched and bound, so that he could not move. Cords were attached to his arms and legs, and then connected with a windlass, which, when turned, dislocated the joints of the wrists and ankles.

The *strappado* or vertical rack was no less painful. The prisoner with his hands tied behind his back was raised by a rope attached to a pulley and windlass to the top of a gallows, or to the ceiling of the torture chamber; he was then let fall with a jerk to within a few inches of the ground. This was repeated several times. The cruel torturers sometimes tied weights to the victim's feet to increase the shock of the fall.

[1] Lea, *op. cit.*, vol. i, p. 421.
[2] Douais, *Documents*, vol. i, p. ccxl.
[3] Douais, *Documents*, vol. ii, p. 115 and seq.

The punishment of burning, "although a very dangerous punishment," as an Inquisitor informs us, was occasionally used. We read of an official of Poitiers, who, following a Toulousain custom, tortured a sorceress by placing her feet on burning coals (*juxta carbones accensos*). This punishment is described by Marsollier in his *Histoire de l'Inquisition*. First a good fire was started; then the victim was stretched out on the ground, his feet manacled, and turned toward the flame. Grease, fat, or some other combustible substance was rubbed upon them, so that they were horribly burned. From time to time a screen was placed between the victim's feet and the brazier, that the Inquisitor might have an opportunity to resume his interrogatory.

Such methods of torturing the accused were so detestable, that in the beginning the torturer was always a civil official, as we read in the bull of Innocent IV. The canons of the Church, moreover, prohibited all ecclesiastics from taking part in these tortures, so that the Inquisitor who, for whatever reason, accompanied the victim into the torture chamber, was thereby rendered irregular, and could not exercise his office again, until he had obtained the necessary dispensation. The tribunals complained of this cumbrous mode of administration, and declared that it hindered them from properly interrogating the accused. Every effort was made to have the prohibition against clerics being present in the torture chamber removed. Their object was at last obtained indirectly. On April 27, 1260, Alexander IV authorized the Inquisitors and their associates to mutually grant all the needed dispensations for irregularities that might be in-

THE INQUISITION

curred.[1] This permission was granted a second time by Urban IV, August 4, 1262;[2] it was practically an authorization to assist at the interrogatories at which torture was employed. From this time the Inquisitors did not scruple to appear in person in the torture chamber. The manuals of the Inquisition record this practice and approve it.[3]

Torture was not to be employed until the judge had been convinced that gentle means were of no avail.[4] Even in the torture chamber, while the prisoner was being stripped of his garments and was being bound, the Inquisitor kept urging him to confess his guilt. On his refusal, the *vexatio* began with slight tortures. If these proved ineffectual, others were applied with gradually increased severity; at the very beginning, the victim was shown all the various instruments of torture, in order that the mere sight of them might terrify him into yielding.[5]

The Inquisitors realized so well that such forced confessions were valueless, that they required the prisoner to confirm them after he had left the torture chamber. The torture was not to exceed a half hour. "Usually," writes Lea, "the procedure appears to be that the torture was continued until the accuser signified his readiness to confess, when he was unbound and carried into another room where his confession was made. If, however, the confession was extracted during the torture, it was read over subsequently to

[1] Douais, *Documents*, vol. i, p. xxv, n. 3.
[2] *Regesta*, no. 18390.
[3] Eymeric, *Directorium*, 3ª pars, p. 481.
[4] A grave suspicion against the prisoner was required before he could be tortured.
[5] Eymeric, *Directorium*, 3ª pars, p. 481, col. 1.

the prisoner, and he was asked if it were true. . . . In any case, the record was carefully made that the confession was free and spontaneous, without the pressure of force or fear."[1]

"It is a noteworthy fact, however, that in the fragmentary documents of inquisitorial proceedings which have reached us, the references to torture are singularly few. . . . In the six hundred and thirty-six sentences borne upon the register of Toulouse from 1309 to 1323, the only allusion to torture is in the recital of the case of Calvarie, but there are numerous instances in which the information wrung from the convicts who had no hope of escape, could scarce have been procured in any other manner. Bernard Gui, who conducted the Inquisition of Toulouse during this period, has too emphatically expressed his sense of the utility of torture on both principals and witnesses for us to doubt his readiness in its employment."[2]

Besides, the investigation which Clement V ordered into the iniquities of the Inquisition of Carcassonne, proves clearly that the accused were frequently subjected to torture.[3] That we rarely find reference to torture in the records of the Inquisition need not surprise us. For in the beginning, torture was inflicted by civil executioners outside of the tribunal of the Inquisition; and even later on, when the Inquisitors were allowed to take part in it, it was considered merely a means of making the prisoner declare his

[1] Lea, *op. cit.*, vol. i, p. 427.
[2] Lea, *op. cit.*, p. 424.
[3] Clement V required the consent of the Inquisitor and the local Bishop before a heretic could be tortured, *vel tormentis exponere illis*. Decretal *Multorum querela*, in Eymeric. *Directorium*, 2ª pars, p. 112.

THE INQUISITION 113

willingness to confess afterwards. A confession made under torture had no force in law; the second confession only was considered valid. That is why it alone, as a rule, is recorded.

But if the sufferings of the victims of the Inquisition were not deemed worthy of mention in the records, they were none the less real and severe. Imprudent or heartless judges were guilty of grave abuses in the use of torture. Rome, which had authorized it, at last intervened, not, we regret to say, to prohibit it altogether, but at least to reform the abuses which had been called to her attention. One reform of Clement V ordered the Inquisition never to use torture without the Bishop's consent, if he could be reached within eight days.[1]

"Bernard Gui emphatically remonstrated against this, as seriously crippling the efficiency of the Inquisition, and proposed to substitute for it the meaningless phrase that torture should only be used *with mature and careful deliberation*, but his suggestion was not heeded, and the Clementine regulations remained the law of the Church."[2]

The code of the Inquisition was now practically complete, for succeeding Popes made no change of any importance. The data before us prove that the Church forgot her early traditions of toleration, and borrowed from the Roman jurisprudence, revived by the legists, laws and practices which remind one of the cruelty of ancient paganism. But once this criminal code was adopted, she endeavored to mitigate the

[1] Decretal, *Multorum querela*.
[2] Lea, *op. cit.*, vol. i, p. 424; Bernard Gui, *Practica*, ed. Douais, 4[a] pars, p. 188.

cruelty with which it was enforced. If this preoccupation is not always visible—and it is not in her condemnation of obdurate heretics—we must at least give her the credit of insisting that torture " should never imperil life or injure limb: " *Cogere citra membri diminutionem et mortis periculum.*

We will now ask how the theologians and canonists interpreted this legislation, and how the tribunals of the Inquisition enforced it.

CHAPTER VIII

THEOLOGIANS, CANONISTS, AND CASUISTS OF THE INQUISITION

THE gravity of the crime of heresy was early recognized in the Church. Gratian discussed this question in a special chapter of his *Decretum*.[1] Innocent III, Guala, the Dominican, and the Emperor Frederic II, as we have seen, looked upon heresy as treason against Almighty God, *i. e.*, the most dreadful of crimes.

The theologians, and even the civil authorities, did not concern themselves much with the evil effects of heresy upon the social order, but viewed it rather as an offense against God. Thus they made no distinction between those teachings which entailed injury on the family and on society, and those which merely denied certain revealed truths. Innocent III, in his constitution of September 23, 1207, legislated particularly against the Patarins, but he took care to point out that no heretic, no matter what the nature of his error might be, should be allowed to escape the full penalty of the law.[2] Frederic II spoke in similar terms in his Constitutions of 1220, 1224, and 1232. This was the current teaching throughout the Middle Ages.

[1] *Causa* xxxi, q. vii, cap. 16.   [2] *Ep.* x, 130.

But it is important to know what men then understood by the word heresy. We can ascertain this from the theologians and canonists, especially from St. Raymond of Pennafort and St. Thomas Aquinas. St. Raymond gives four meanings to the word heretic, but from the standpoint of the canon law he says. "A heretic is one who denies the faith." [1] St. Thomas Aquinas is more accurate. He declares that no one is truly a heretic unless he obstinately maintains his error, even after it has been pointed out to him by ecclesiastical authority. This is the teaching of St. Augustine.[2]

But by degrees the word, taken at first in a strict sense, acquired a broader meaning. St. Raymond includes schism in the notion of heresy. "The only difference between these two crimes," he writes, "is the difference between genus and species;" every schism ends in heresy. And relying on the authority of St. Jerome, the rigorous canonist goes so far as to declare that schism is even a greater crime than heresy. He proves this by the fact that Core, Dathan, and Abiron,[3] who seceded from the chosen people, were punished by the most terrible of punishments. "From the enormity of the punishment, must we not argue the enormity of the crime?" St. Raymond therefore declares that the same punishment must be inflicted upon the heretic and the schismatic.[4]

"The authors of the treatises on the Inquisition,"

---

[1] S. Raymundi, *Summa*, lib. i, cap. *De Hœreticis*, sect. i, Roman Edition, 1603, p. 39.

[2] *Summa*, IIa, IIae, quæst. xi, Conclusio; cf. *ibid.*, ad 3um, quotations from St. Augustine.

[3] Num. xvi. 31–33.

[4] *Loc. cit.*, lib. i, cap. *De schismatics*, pp. 45–47.

writes Tanon, "classed as heretics all those who favored heresy, and all excommunicates who did not submit to the Church within a certain period. They declared that a man excommunicated for any cause whatever, who did not seek absolution within a year, incurred by this act of rebellion a light suspicion of heresy; that he could then be cited before the Inquisitor to answer not only for the crime which had caused his excommunication, but also for his orthodoxy. If he did not answer this second summons, he was at once considered excommunicated for heresy, and if he remained under this second excommunication for a year, he was liable to be condemned as a real heretic. The light suspicion caused by his first excommunication became in turn a vehement and then a violent suspicion which, together with his continued contumacy, constituted a full proof of heresy."[1]

The theologians insisted greatly upon respect for ecclesiastical and especially Papal authority. Everything that tended to lessen this authority seemed to them a practical denial of the faith. The canonist Henry of Susa (Hostiensis+1271), went so far as to say that "whoever contradicted or refused to accept the decretals of the Popes was a heretic."[2] Such disobedience was looked upon as a culpable disregard of the rights of the papacy, and consequently a form of heresy.

Superstition was also classed under the heading of heresy. The canonist Zanchino Ugolini tells us that he was present at the condemnation of an immoral priest, who was punished by the Inquisitors not for

[1] Tanon, *op. cit.*, pp. 235, 236.
[2] In Baluze-Mansi, *Miscellanea*, vol. ii, p. 275.

his licentiousness, but because he said Mass every day in a state of sin, and urged in excuse that he considered himself pardoned by the mere fact of putting on the sacred vestments.[1]

The Jews, as such, were never regarded as heretics. But the usury they so widely practiced evidenced an unorthodox doctrine on thievery, which made them liable to be suspected of heresy. Indeed, we find several Popes upbraiding them " for maintaining that usury is not a sin." Some Christians also fell into the same error, and thereby became subject to the Inquisition. Pope Martin V, in his bull of November 6, 1419, authorizes the Inquisitors to prosecute these usurers.[2]

Sorcery and magic were also put on a par with heresy. Pope Alexander IV had decided that divination and sorcery did not fall under the jurisdiction of the Inquisition, unless there was manifest heresy involved.[3] But casuists were not wanting to prove that heresy was involved in such cases. The belief in the witches' nightly rides through the air, led by Diana or Herodias of Palestine, was very widespread in the Middle Ages, and was held by some as late as the fifteenth century. The question whether the devil could carry off men and women was warmly debated by the theologians of the time. " A case adduced by Albertus Magnus, in a disputation on the subject before the Bishop of Paris, and recorded by Thomas of Cantimpré, in which the daughter of the Count of Schwalenberg was regularly carried away every night

---

[1] *Tractat, de Hæret.*, cap. ii.
[2] Bull *Inter cætera*, sent to the Inquisitor Pons Feugeyron.
[3] Bull of December 9, 1257.

for several hours, gave immense satisfaction to the adherents of the new doctrine, and eventually an ample store of more modern instances was accumulated to confirm Satan in his enlarged privileges."[1] Satan, it seems, imprinted upon his clients an indelible mark, the *stigma diabolicum*.

"In 1458, the Inquisitor Nicholas Jaquerius remarked reasonably enough that even if the affair was an illusion, it was none the less heretical, as the followers of Diana and Herodias were necessarily heretics in their waking hours."[2]

About 1250, the Inquisitor Bernard of Como taught categorically that the phenomena of witchcraft, especially the attendance at the witches' Sabbat, were not fanciful but real: "This is proved," he says, "from the fact that the Popes permitted witches to be burned at the stake; they would not have countenanced this, if these persons were not real heretics, and their crimes only imaginary, for the Church only punishes proved crimes."[3] Witchcraft was, therefore, amenable to the tribunals of the Inquisition.[4]

While the casuists thus increased the number of crimes which the Inquisition could prosecute, on the other hand, they shortened the judicial procedure then in vogue.

Following the Roman law, the Inquisition at first recognized three forms of action in criminal cases—

[1] Lea, *op. cit.*, vol. iii, p. 497.
[2] Lea, *op. cit.*, pp. 497, 498.
[3] *Lucerna Inquisitorium*, Romæ, 1584, p. 144.
[4] In a letter of one of the cardinals of the Holy Office, dated 1643, witchcraft is classed with heresy. Douais, *Documents*, vol. i, p. ccliv. In practice, the heretical tendency of witchcraft was hard to determine. Each judge, therefore, as a rule, pronounced sentence according to his own judgment.

accusatio, denuntiatio, and *inquisitio.* In the *accusatio,* the accuser formally inscribed himself as able to prove his accusation; if he failed to do so, he had to undergo the penalty which the prisoner would have incurred (*pœna talionis*).[1] " From the very beginning, he was placed in the same position as the one he accused, even to the extent of sharing his imprisonment."[2] The *denuntiatio* did not in any way bind the accuser; he merely handed in his testimony, and then ceased prosecuting the case; the judge at once proceeded to take action against the accused. In the *inquisitio,* there was no one either to accuse or denounce the criminal; the judge cited the suspected criminal before him and proceeded to try him. This was the most common method of procedure; from it the Inquisition received its name.[3]

The Inquisitorial procedure was therefore inspired by the Roman law. But in practice the *accusatio,* which gave the prisoner a chance to meet the charges against him, was soon abandoned. In fact the Inquisitors were always most anxious to set it aside. Urban IV enacted a decree, July 28, 1262, whereby they were allowed to proceed *simpliciter et de plano, absque advocatorum strepitu et figura.*[4] Bernard Gui insisted on this in his *Practica.*[5] Eymeric advised his associates, when an accuser appeared before them who was perfectly willing to accept the *pœna talionis* in case of failure, to urge the imprudent man to withdraw

[1] Tanon, *op. cit.,* p. 260, n. 4.
[2] Tancrède, *Ordo judiciorum,* lib. ii.
[3] On these three forms of action, cf. Eymeric, *Directorium,* 3ᵃ pars, p. 413 et seq.
[4] Bull *Præ cunctis* of July 28, 1262.
[5] *Practica,* 4ᵃ pars, ed. Douais, p. 192.

his demand. For he argued that the *accusatio* might prove harmful to himself, and besides give too much room for trickery.[1] In other words, the Inquisitors wished to be perfectly untrammeled in their action.

The secrecy of the Inquisition's procedure was one of the chief causes of complaint.

But the Inquisition, dreadful as it was, did not lack defenders. Some of their arguments were most extravagant and far-fetched. " Paramo, in the quaint pedantry with which he ingeniously proves that God was the first Inquisitor, and the condemnation of Adam and Eve the first model of the Inquisitorial process, triumphantly points out that he judges them in secret, thus setting the example which the Inquisition is bound to follow, and avoiding the subtleties which the criminals would have raised in their defence, especially at the suggestion of the crafty serpent. That he called no witnesses is explained by the confession of the accused, and ample legal authority is cited to show that these confessions were sufficient to justify the conviction and punishment." [2]

. . . .

The subtlety of the casuists had full play when they came to discuss the torture of the prisoner who absolutely refused to confess. According to law, the torture could be inflicted but once, but this regulation was easily evaded. For it was lawful to subject the prisoner to all the various kinds of torture in succession; and if additional evidence were discovered, the torture could be repeated. When they desired, therefore, to repeat the torture, even after an interval of

[1] *Directorium*, p. 414, col. 1.
[2] Lea, *op. cit.*, vol. i, p. 406.

some days, they evaded the law by calling it technically not a "repetition" but a "continuance of the first torture:" *Ad continuandum tormenta, non ad iterandum*, as Eymeric styles it.[1] This quibbling of course gave full scope to the cruelty and the indiscreet zeal of the Inquisitors.

But a new difficulty soon arose. Confessions extorted under torture, had, as we have seen, no legal value. Eymeric himself admitted that the results obtained in this way were very unreliable, and that the Inquisitors should realize this fact.

If, on leaving the torture chamber, the prisoner reiterated his confession, the case was at once decided. But suppose, on the contrary, that the confession extorted under torture was afterwards retracted, what was to be done? The Inquisitors did not agree upon this point. Some of them, like Eymeric, held that in this case the prisoner was entitled to his freedom. Others, like the author of the *Sacro Arsenale*, held that " the torture should be repeated, in order that the prisoner might be forced to reiterate his first confession which had evidently compromised him." This seems to have been the traditional practice of the Italian tribunals.

But the casuists did not stop here. They discovered " that Clement V had only spoken of torture in general, and had not specifically alluded to witnesses, whence they concluded that one of the most shocking abuses of the system, the torture of witnesses, was left to the sole discretion of the Inquisitor, and this became the accepted rule. It only required an additional step to show that after the accused had been convicted by

[1] Eymeric, *Directorium*, 3ª pars, p. 481, col. 2.

evidence or had confessed as to himself, he became a witness as to the guilt of his friends, and thus could be arbitrarily (?) tortured to betray them."[1]

. . . .

As a matter of course, the canonists and the theologians approved the severest penalties inflicted by the Inquisition. St. Raymond of Pennafort, however, who was one of the most favored counsellors of Gregory IX, still upheld the criminal code of Innocent III. The severest penalties he defended were the excommunication of heretics and schismatics, their banishment and the confiscation of their property.[2] His *Summa* was undoubtedly completed when the Decretal of Gregory IX appeared, authorizing the Inquisitors to enforce the cruel laws of Frederic II.

But St. Thomas, who wrote at a time when the Inquisition was in full operation, felt called upon to defend the infliction of the death penalty upon heretics and the relapsed. His words deserve careful con-

[1] Lea, *op. cit.*, vol. i, p. 425.

[2] Lea writes (*op. cit.*, vol. i, p. 229, note): "Saint Raymond of Pennafort, the compiler of the decretals of Gregory IX, who was the highest authority in his generation, lays it down as a principle of ecclesiastical law that the heretic is to be coerced by excommunication and confiscation, and if they fail, *by the extreme exercise of the secular power*. The man who was doubtful in faith was to be held a heretic, and so also was the schismatic who, while believing all the articles of religion, refused the obedience due to the Roman Church. All alike were to be forced into the Roman fold, and the fate of Core, Dathan and Abiron was invoked *for the destruction of the obstinate*." (*Summa*, lib. i, tit. v, 2, 4, 8; tit. vi, i.) This is a travesty of the mind, and words of Saint Raymond. He merely called attention to the lot of Core, Dathan and Abiron to show what a great crime schism was. He never asserted that heretics or schismatics, even when obdurate, ought to be "destroyed." *Summa*, lib. i, cap. *De Hæreticis* and *De Schismaticis*.

sideration. He begins by answering the objections that might be brought from the Scriptures and the Fathers against his thesis. The first of these is the well-known passage of St. Matthew, in which our Saviour forbids the servants of the householder to gather up the cockle before the harvest time, lest they root up the wheat with it.[1] St. John Chrysostom, he says, " argues from this text that it is wrong to put heretics to death." [2] But according to St. Augustine the words of the Saviour: " Let the cockle grow until the harvest," are explained at once by what follows: "lest perhaps gathering up the cockle, you root up the wheat also with it." When there is no danger of uprooting the wheat and no danger of schism, violent measures may be used: *Cum metus iste non subest . . . non dormiat severitas disciplinæ.*[3] We doubt very much whether such reasoning would have satisfied St. John Chrysostom, St. Theodore the Studite, or Bishop Wazo, who understood the Saviour's prohibition in a literal and an absolute sense.

But this passage does not reveal the whole mind of the Angelic doctor. It is more evident in his exegesis of Ezechiel xviii. 32, *Nolo mortem peccatoris.* " Assuredly," he writes, " none of us desires the death of a single heretic. But remember that the house of David could not obtain peace until Absalom was killed in the war he waged against his father. In like manner, the Catholic Church saves some of her children by the death of others, and consoles her sorrowing heart by reflecting that she is acting for the general good." [4]

[1] Matt. xiii. 28-30.
[2] *In Matthæum*, Homil. xlvi.
[3] Augustine, *Contra epistol. Parmeniani*, lib. iii, cap. ii.
[4] St. Thomas, *Summa, loc. cit.*, ad. 4m.

If we are not mistaken, St. Thomas is here trying to prove, on the authority of St. Augustine, that it is sometimes lawful to put heretics to death.

But it is only by garbling and distorting the context that St. Thomas makes the Bishop of Hippo advocate the very penalty which, as a matter of fact, he always denounced most strongly. In the passage quoted, St. Augustine was speaking of the benefit that ensues to the Church *from the suicide of heretics*, but he had no idea whatever of maintaining that the Church had the right to put to death her rebellious children.[1] St. Thomas misses the point entirely, and gives his readers a false idea of the teaching of St. Augustine.

Thinking, however, that he has satisfactorily answered all the objections against his thesis, he states it as follows: "Heretics who persist in their error after a second admonition ought not only to be excommunicated, but also abandoned to the secular arm to be put to death. For, he argues, it is much more wicked to corrupt the faith on which depends the life of the soul, than to debase the coinage which provides merely for temporal life; wherefore, if coiners and other malefactors are justly doomed to death, much more may heretics be justly slain once they are convicted. If, therefore, they persist in their error after two admonitions, the Church despairs of their conversion, and excommunicates them to ensure the salvation of others whom they might corrupt; she then abandons them to the secular arm that they may be put to death."[2]

St. Thomas in this passage makes a mere comparison

[1] *Ep.* clxxxv, ad *Bonifacium*, no. 32.
[2] *Summa*, IIa IIae, quæst. xi, art. 3.

serve as an argument. He does not seem to realize that if his reasoning were valid, the Church could go a great deal further, and have the death penalty inflicted in many other cases.

The fate of the relapsed heretic had varied from Lucius III to Alexander IV. The bull *Ad Abolendam* decreed that converted heretics who relapsed into heresy were to be abandoned to the secular arm without trial.[1] But at the time this Decretal was published, the *Animadversio debita* of the State entailed no severer penalty than banishment and confiscation. When this term, already fearful enough, came to mean the death penalty, the Inquisitors did not know whether to follow the ancient custom or to adopt the new interpretation. For a long time they followed the traditional custom. Bernard of Caux, who was undoubtedly a zealous Inquisitor, is a case in point. In his register of sentences from 1244 to 1248, we meet with sixty cases of relapse, not one of whom was punished by a penalty severer than imprisonment. But a little later on the strict interpretation of the *Animadversio debita* began to prevail. In St. Thomas's time it meant the death penalty; and we find him citing the bull *Ad Abolendam*[2] as his authority for the infliction of the death penalty upon the relapsed, penitent or impenitent, in ignorance of the fact that this document originally had a totally different interpretation.

His reasoning therefore rests on a false supposition. He advocates the death penalty for the relapsed in the name of Christian charity. For, he argues, charity

---

[1] Decretals, in cap. ix, *De hæreticis*, lib. v, tit. vii.
[2] *Summa*, IIa IIae, quæst. ix, art. 4: *Sed contra*.

has for its object the spiritual and temporal welfare of one's neighbor. His spiritual welfare is the salvation of his soul; his temporal welfare is life, and temporal advantages, such as riches, dignities, and the like. These temporal advantages are subordinate to the spiritual, and charity must prevent their endangering the eternal salvation of their possessor. Charity, therefore, to himself and to others, prompts us to deprive him of these temporal goods, if he makes a bad use of them. For if we allowed the relapsed heretic to live, we would undoubtedly endanger the salvation of others, either because he would corrupt the faithful whom he met, or because his escape from punishment would lead others to believe they could deny the faith with impunity. The inconstancy of the relapsed is, therefore, a sufficient reason why the Church, although she receives him to penance for his soul's salvation, refuses to free him from the death penalty.

Such reasoning is not very convincing. Why would not the life imprisonment of the heretic safeguard the faithful as well as his death? Will you answer that this penalty is too trivial to prevent the faithful from falling into heresy? If that be so, why not at once condemn all heretics to death, even when repentant? That would terrorize the wavering ones all the more. But St. Thomas evidently was not thinking of the logical consequences of his reasoning. His one aim was to defend the criminal code in vogue at the time. That is his only excuse. For we must admit that rarely has his reasoning been so faulty and so weak as in his thesis upon the coercive power of the Church, and the punishment of heresy.

.   .   .   .

St. Thomas defended the death penalty without indicating how it was to be inflicted. The commentators who followed him were more definite. The *Animadversio debita*, says Henry of Susa (Hostiensis+ 1271), in his commentary on the bull *Ad Abolendam*, is the penalty of the stake (*ignis crematio*). He defends this interpretation by quoting the words of Christ: "If any one abide not in me, he shall be cast forth as a branch, and shall wither, and they shall gather him *and cast him into the fire,* and he *burneth.* "[1] Jean d'Andre (+1348), whose commentary carried equal weight with Henry of Susa's throughout the Middle Ages, quotes the same text as authority for sending heretics to the stake.[2] According to this peculiar exegesis, the law and custom of the day merely sanctioned the law of Christ. To regard our Saviour as the precursor or rather the author of the criminal code of the Inquisition evidences, one must admit, a very peculiar temper of mind.

. . . .

The next step was to free the Church from all responsibility in the infliction of the death penalty— truly an extremely difficult undertaking.

St. Thomas held, with many other theologians, that heretics condemned by the Inquisition should be abandoned to the secular arm, *judicio sæculari*. But he went further, and declared it the duty of the State to put such criminals to death.[3] The State, therefore,

---

[1] John, xv, 6; Hostiensis, on the decretal *Ad Abolendum*, cap. xi, in Eymeric, *Directorium inquisitorum*, 2ª pars, pp. 149, 150.

[2] On the decretal *Ad Abolendum*, cap. xiv, in Eymeric, *ibid.*, pp. 170. 171,

[3] *Summa*, IIa, IIae, quæst. xi, art. 3.

THE INQUISITION 129

was to carry out this sentence at least indirectly in the name of the Church.

A contemporary of St. Thomas thus meets this difficulty: "The Pope does not execute any one," he says, "or order him to be put to death; heretics are executed by the law which the Pope tolerates; they practically cause their own death by committing crimes which merit death."[1] The heretic who received this answer to his objections must surely have found it very farfetched. He could easily have replied that the Pope "not only allowed heretics to be put to death, but ordered this done under penalty of excommunication." And by this very fact he incurred all the odium of the death penalty.

The casuists of the Inquisition, however, came to the rescue, and tried to defend the Church by another subterfuge. They denounced in so many words the death penalty and other similar punishments, while at the same time they insisted upon the State's enforcing them. The formula by which they dismissed an impenitent or a relapsed heretic was thus worded: "We dismiss you from our ecclesiastical forum, and abandon you to the secular arm. But we strongly beseech the secular court to mitigate its sentence in such a way as to avoid bloodshed or danger of death."[2] We regret to state, however, that the civil judges were not supposed to take these words literally. If they were at all inclined to do so, they would have been quickly called to a sense of their duty by being excommunicated. The clause inserted by the canonists was a

[1] *Disputatio inter catholicum et Paterinum hæreticum*, cap. xii, in Martène, *Thesaurus Anecdotorum*, vol. v, col. 1741.
[2] Eymeric, *Directorium inquisitorum*, 3 pars, p. 515, col. 2.

mere legal fiction, which did not change matters a particle.

It is hard to understand why such a formula was used at all. Probably it was first used in other criminal cases in which abandonment to the secular arm did not imply the death penalty, and the Inquisition kept using it merely out of respect to tradition. It seemed to palliate the too flagrant contradiction which existed between ecclesiastical justice and the teaching of Christ, and it gave at least an external homage to the teaching of St. Augustine, and the first Fathers of the Church. Moreover, as it furnished a specious means of evading by the merest form of prohibition against clerics taking part in sentences involving the effusion of blood and death, and the irregularity resulting therefrom, the Inquisitors used it to reassure their conscience.

Finally, however, some Inquisitors, realizing the emptiness of this formula, dispensed with it altogether, and boldly assumed the full responsibility for their sentences. They deemed the rôle of the State so unimportant in the execution of heretics, that they did not even mention it. The Inquisition is the real judge; it lights the fires. "All whom we cause to be burned," says the famous Dominican Sprenger in his *Malleus Maleficarum*.[1] Although not intended as an accurate statement of fact,[2] it indicates pretty well the current

[1] *Malleus maleficarum maleficas et earum hæresim framea conterens*, auct. Jacobo Sprengero, Lugduni, 1660, pars ii, quæst. i, cap. ii, p. 108, col. 2.

[2] We must interpret in the same sense the decree of the Council of Constance pronouncing the penalty of the stake against the followers of John Huss, John Wyclif and Jerome of Prague. Session xliv, no. 23, Harduin, *Concilia*, vol. viii, col. 896 et

idea regarding the share of the ecclesiastical tribunals in the punishment of heretics.

. . . .

It is evident that the theologians and canonists were simply apologists for the Inquisition, and interpreters of its laws. As a rule, they tried, like St. Raymond Pennafort and St. Thomas, to defend the decrees of the Popes. We cannot say that they succeeded in their task. Some by their untimely zeal rather compromised the cause they endeavored to defend. Others, going counter to the canon law, drew conclusions from it that the Popes never dreamed of, and in this way made the procedure of the Inquisition, already severe enough, still more severe, especially in the use of torture.

seq. The Council here indicates only the usual punishment for the relapsed, without really decreeing it.

CHAPTER IX

The Inquisition in Operation

We do not intend to relate every detail of the Inquisition's action. A brief outline, a sort of bird's-eye view, will suffice.

Its field, although very extensive, did not comprise the whole of Christendom, nor even all the Latin countries. The Scandinavian kingdoms escaped it almost entirely; England experienced it only once in the case of the Templars; Castile and Portugal knew nothing of it before the reign of Ferdinand and Isabella. It was almost unknown in France—at least as an established institution—except in the South, in what was called the county of Toulouse, and later on in Languedoc.

The Inquisition was in full operation in Aragon. The Cathari, it seems, were wont to travel frequently from Languedoc to Lombardy, so that upper Italy had from an early period its contingent of Inquisitors. Frederic II had it established in the two Sicilies and in many cities of Italy and Germany. Honorius IV (1285-1287) introduced it into Sardinia.[1] Its activity in Flanders and Bohemia in the fifteenth century was very considerable. These were the chief centers of its operations.

[1] Potthast, no. 22307; *Registres d'Honorius IV*, published by Maurice Prou, 1888, no. 163.

Some of the Inquisitors had an exalted idea of their office. We recall the ideal portrait of the perfect Inquisitor drawn by Bernard Gui and Eymeric. But, by an inevitable law of history, the reality never comes up to the ideal.

We know the names of many Inquisitors, monks and bishops.[1] There are some whose memory is beyond reproach; in fact the Church honors them as saints, because they died for the faith.[2]

But others fulfilled the duties of their office in a spirit of hatred and impatience, contrary both to natural justice and to Christian charity. Who can help denouncing, for instance, the outrageous conduct of Conrad of Marburg. Contemporary writers tell us that when heretics appeared before his tribunal, he granted them no delay, but at once required them to answer yes or no to the accusations against them. If they confessed their guilt, they were granted their lives, and thrown into prison; if they refused to confess, they were at once condemned and sent to the stake. Such summary justice strongly resembles injustice.

But Robert the Dominican, known as Robert the Bougre, for he was a converted Patarin, surpassed even Conrad in cruelty. Among the exploits of this Inquisitor, special mention must be made of the executions at Montwimer in Champagne. The Bishop, Moranis, had allowed a large community of heretics to grow up about him. Robert determined to punish the town severely. In one week he managed to try all his prisoners. On May 29, 1239, about one hundred

[1] Mgr. Douais, *Documents*, vol. i, pp. cxxix–ccix.
[2] *V. g.*, Peter of Verona, assassinated by heretics in 1252.

and eighty of them, with their bishop, were sent to the stake. Such summary proceedings caused complaints to be sent to Rome against this cruel Inquisitor. He was accused of confounding in his blind fanaticism the innocent with the guilty, and of working upon simple souls so as to increase the number of his victims. An investigation proved that these complaints were well founded. In fact, it revealed such outrages that Robert the Bougre was at first suspended from his office, and finally condemned to perpetual imprisonment.[1]

Other acts of the Inquisition were no less odious. In 1280 the Consuls of Carcassonne complained to the Pope, the King of France, and the episcopal vicars of the diocese of the cruelty and injustice of Jean Galand in the use of torture. He had inscribed on the walls of the Inquisition these words: *domunculas ad torquendum et cruciandum homines diversis generibus tormentorum*. Some prisoners had been tortured on the rack, and most of them were so cruelly treated that they lost the use of their arms and legs, and became altogether helpless. Some even died in great agony of their torments. The complaint continues in this tone, and mentions five or six times the great cruelty of the tortures inflicted.

Philip the Fair, who was noble-hearted occasionally, addressed a letter May 13, 1291, to the seneschal of Carcassonne in which he denounced the Inquisitors for their cruel torturing of innocent men, whereby the living and the dead were fraudulently convicted; and among other abuses he mentions particularly " tor-

[1] Aubri des Trois Fontaines, ad ann. 1239, *Mon. Germ., SS.*, vol. xxiii, 944, 945.

tures newly invented." Another letter of his (1301) addressed to Foulques de Saint-Georges, contained a similar denunciation.

In a bull intended for Cardinals Taillefer de la Chappelle and Bérenger de Frédol, March 13, 1306, Clement V mentions the complaints of the citizens of Carcassonne, Albi, and Cordes, regarding the cruelty practiced in the prisons of the Inquisition. Several of these unfortunates " were so weakened by the rigors of their imprisonment, the lack of food, and the severity of their tortures (*sevitia tormentorum*), that they died."

The facts in Savonarola's case are very hard to determine. The official account of his interrogatory declares that he was subjected to three and a half *tratti di fune*. This was a form of torture known as the *strappado*. The Signoria, in answer to the reproaches of Alexander VI at their tardiness, declared that they had to deal with a man of great endurance; that they had assiduously tortured him for many days with slender results.[1] Burchard, the papal prothonotary, states that he was put to the torture seven times. It made very little difference whether these tortures were inflicted *per modum continuationis* or *per modum iterationis*, as the casuist of the Inquisition put it. At any rate, it was a crying abuse.[2]

We may learn something of the brutality of the Inquisitors from the remorse felt by one of them. He had inflicted the torture of the burning coals upon a sorceress. The unfortunate woman died soon after-

[1] Villari, *La storia di Girolamo Savonarola*, Firenze, 1887, vol. ii, p. 197.
[2] H. Lucas, *Fra Girolamo Savonarola, a Biographical Study*. London, Sands, 1905.

wards in prison as a result of her torments. The Inquisitor, knowing he had caused her death, wrote John XXII for dispensation from the irregularity he had thereby incurred.

But the greatest excesses of the Inquisition were due to the political schemes of sovereigns. Such instances were by no means rare. Hardly had the Inquisition been established, when Frederic II tried to use it for political purposes. He was anxious to put the prosecution for heresy in the hands of his royal officers, rather than in the hands of the bishops and the monks. When, therefore, in 1233, he boasted in a letter to Gregory IX that he had put to death a great number of heretics in his kingdom, the Pope answered that he was not at all deceived by this pretended zeal. He knew full well that the Emperor wished simply to get rid of his personal enemies, and that he had put to death many who were not heretics at all.

The personal interests of Philip the Fair were chiefly responsible for the trial and condemnation of the Templars. Clement V himself and the ecclesiastical judges were both unfortunately guilty of truckling in the whole affair. But their unjust condemnation was due chiefly to the king's desire to confiscate their great possessions.[1]

[1] The tribunals of the Inquisition were perhaps never more cruel than in the case of the Templars. At Paris, according to the testimony of Ponsard de Gisiac, thirty-six Templars perished under torture. At Sens, Jacques de Saciac said that twenty-five had died of torment and suffering. (Lea, *op. cit.*, vol. iii, p. 262.) The Grand Master, Jacques Molay, owed his life to the vigor of his constitution. Confessions extorted by such means were altogether valueless. Despite all his efforts, Philip the Fair never succeeded in obtaining a formal condemnation of the Order.

Joan of Arc was also a victim demanded by the political interests of the day. If the Bishop of Beauvais, Pierre Cauchon, had not been such a bitter English partisan, it is very probable that the tribunal over which he presided would not have brought in the verdict of guilty, which sent her to the stake;[1] she would never have been considered a heretic at all, much less a relapsed one.

It would be easy to cite many instances of the same. kind, especially in Spain. If there was any place in the world where the State interfered unjustly in the trials of the Inquisition, it was in the kingdom of Ferdinand and Isabella, the kingdom of Philip II.[2]

From all that has been said, we must not infer that the tribunals of the Inquisition were always guilty of cruelty and injustice; we ought simply to conclude that too frequently they were. Even one case of brutality and injustice deserves perpetual odium.

. . . .

The severest penalties the Inquisition could inflict (apart from the minor penalties of pilgrimages, wearing the crosses, etc.), were imprisonment, abandonment to the secular arm, and confiscation of property.

" Imprisonment, according to the theory of the Inquisition, was not a punishment, but a means by which

---

[1] The greatest crime of the trial was the substitution, in the documents, of a different form of abjuration from the one Joan read near the church of Saint-Ouen.

[2] The complaints of various Popes proves this. Cf. Héféle, *Le Cardinal Ximénes*, Paris, 1857, pp. 265-374. Langlois, *L'Inquisition d'après les travaux recents*, Paris, 1902, pp. 89-141; Bernaldez, *Historia de los Reyes: Cronicas de los reyes de Castilla, Fernandez y Isabel*, Madrid, 1878; Rodrigo, *Historia verdadera de la Inquisicion*, 3 vol., Madrid, 1876-1877.

the penitent could obtain, on the bread of tribulation and the water of affliction, pardon from God for his sins, while at the same time he was closely supervised to see that he persevered in the right path, and was segregated from the rest of the flock, thus removing all danger of infection." [1]

Heretics who confessed their errors during the time of grace were imprisoned only for a short time; those who confessed under torture or under threat of death were imprisoned for life; this was the usual punishment for the relapsed during most of the thirteenth century. It was the only penalty that Bernard of Caux (1244–1248) inflicted upon them.

"There were two kinds of imprisonment," writes Lea, "the milder or *murus largus*, and the harsher, known as *murus strictus*, or *durus*, or *arctus*. All were on bread and water, and the confinement, according to rule, was solitary, each penitent in a separate cell, with no access allowed to him, to prevent his being corrupted, or corrupting others; but this could not be strictly enforced, and about 1306 Geoffroi d'Ablis stigmatizes as an abuse the visits of clergy and the laity of both sexes, permitted to prisoners." [2]

As far back as 1282, Jean Galand had forbidden the jailer of the prison of Carcassonne to eat or take recreation with the prisoners, or to allow them to take recreation, or to keep servants.

Husband and wife, however, were allowed access to each other if either or both were imprisoned; and late in the fourteenth century Eymeric declared that zealous Catholics might be admitted to visit prisoners, but

[1] Lea, *op. cit.*, vol. i, p. 484.
[2] Lea, *op. cit.*, vol. i, pp. 486, 487.

THE INQUISITION

not women and simple folk who might be perverted, for converted prisoners, he added, were very liable to relapse, and to infect others, and usually died at the stake.[1]

"In the milder form, or *murus largus*, the prisoners apparently were, if well behaved, allowed to take exercise in the corridors, where sometimes they had opportunities of converse with each other, and with the outside world. This privilege was ordered to be given to the aged and infirm by the cardinals who investigated the prison of Carcassonne, and took measures to alleviate its rigors. In the harsher confinement, or *murus strictus*, the prisoner was thrust into the smallest, darkest, and most noisome of cells, with chains on his feet,—in some cases chained to the wall. This penance was inflicted on those whose offences had been conspicuous, or who had perjured themselves by making incomplete confessions, the matter being wholly at the discretion of the Inquisitor. I have met with one case, in 1328, of aggravated false-witness, condemned to the *murus strictissimus*, with chains on both hands and feet. When the culprits were members of a religious order, to avoid scandal, the proceedings were usually held in private, and the imprisonment would be ordered to take place in a convent of their own order. As these buildings, however, were unprovided with cells for the punishment of offenders, this was probably of no great advantage to the victim. In the case of Jeanne, widow of B. de la Tour, a nun of Lespinasse, in 1246, who had committed acts of both Catharan and Waldensian heresy, and had prevaricated in her confession, the sentence

[1] Eymeric, *Directorium*, p. 507.

was confinement in a separate cell in her own convent, where no one was to enter or see her, her food being pushed in through an opening left for the purpose—in fact, the living tomb known as the *in pace*." [1]

In these wretched prisons the diet was most meager. But " while the penance prescribed was a diet of bread and water, the Inquisition, with unwonted kindness, did not object to its prisoners receiving from their friends contributions of food, wine, money, and garments, and among its documents are such frequent allusions to this that it may be regarded as an established custom." [2]

The number of prisoners, even with a life sentence, was rather considerable. The collections of sentences that we possess give us precise information on this point.

We have, for instance, the register of Bernard of Caux, the Inquisitor of Toulouse for the years 1244–1246. Out of fifty-two of his sentences, twenty-seven heretics were sentenced to life imprisonment. We must not forget also that several of them contain condemnations of many individuals; the second, for instance, condemned thirty-three persons, twelve of whom were to be imprisoned for life; the fourth condemned eighteen persons to life imprisonment. On the other hand, the register does not record one case of abandonment to the secular arm, even for relapse into heresy.[3]

Bernard must be considered a severe Inquisitor. The register of the notary of Carcassonne, published

[1] Lea, *op. cit.*, vol. i, p. 487.
[2] Lea, *op. cit.*, vol. i, p. 491.
[3] Douais, *Documents*, vol. i, pp. cclx–cclxi; vol. ii, pp. i–89.

by Mgr. Douais, contains for the years 1249–1255 two hundred and seventy-eight articles. But imprisonment very rarely figured among the penances inflicted. The usual penalty was enforced service in the Holy Land, *passagium, transitus ultramarinus*.[1]

Bernard Gui, Inquisitor at Toulouse for seventeen years (1308–1325), was called upon to condemn nine hundred and thirty heretics, of whom two were guilty of false witness, eighty-nine were dead, and forty were fugitives. In the eighteen *Sermones* or *Autos-da-fé* in which he rendered the sentences we possess today, he condemned three hundred and seven to prison, *i. e.*, about one-third of all the heretics brought before his tribunal.[2]

The tribunal of the Inquisition of Pamiers in the *Sermones* of 1318–1324, held ninety-eight heresy trials. The records declare that two were acquitted; and say nothing of the penalty inflicted upon twenty-one others who were tried. The most common penalty was life imprisonment. In the *Sermo* of March 8, thirteen heretics were sentenced to prison, eight of whom were set at liberty on July 4, 1322; these latter were condemned to wear single or double crosses. Six out of ten, tried on August 2, 1321, were sentenced for life to the German prison. On June 19, 1323, six out of ten tried were condemned to prison (*murus strictus*); on August 12, 1324, ten out of eleven tried were condemned for life to the strict prison: *ad strictum muri Carcassonne inquisitionis carcerem in vinculis ferreis ac*

[1] Douais, *Documents*, vol. i, pp. cclxvii–cclxxxiv; vol. ii, pp. 115, 243.

[2] Douais, *Documents*, vol. i, pp. ccv, cf. Appendix B.

Note that the register records 930 condemnations. Cf. Lea, *op. cit.*, vol. i, p. 550.

in pane et aqua. We gather from these statistics that the Inquisition of Pamiers inflicted the penalty of life imprisonment as often as, if not more than, the Inquisition of Toulouse.

We have seen above that the penalty of imprisonment was sometimes mitigated and even commuted. Life imprisonment was sometimes commuted into temporary imprisonment, and both into pilgrimages or wearing the cross. Twenty, imprisoned by the Inquisition of Pamiers, were set at liberty on condition that they wore the cross. This clemency was not peculiar to the Inquisition of Pamiers. In 1328, by a single sentence, twenty-three prisoners of Carcassonne were set at liberty, and other slight penances substituted.

In Bernard Gui's register of sentences we read of one hundred and nineteen cases of release from prison with the obligation to wear the cross, and, of this number, fifty-one were subsequently released from even the minor penalty. Prisoners were sometimes set at liberty on account of sickness, *v. g.*, women with child, or to provide for their families.

"In 1246 we find Bernard de Caux, in sentencing Bernard Sabbatier, a relapsed heretic, to perpetual imprisonment, adding that as the culprit's father is a good Catholic, and old and sick, the son may remain with him, and support him as long as he lives, meanwhile wearing the crosses."[1]

Assuredly this penalty of imprisonment was terrible, but while we may denounce some Inquisitors for having made its suffering more intense out of malice

[1] Lea, *op. cit.*, vol. i, 486.

THE INQUISITION 143

or indifference, we must also admit that others sometimes mitigated its severity.

. . . .

The condemnation of obstinate heretics, and later on, of the relapsed, permitted no exercise of clemency. How many heretics were abandoned to the secular arm, and thus sent to the stake, is impossible to determine. However, we have some interesting statistics of the more important tribunals on this point. The portion of the register of Bernard de Caux which relates to impenitent heretics has been lost, but we have the sentences of the Inquisition of Pamiers (1318–1324), and of Toulouse (1308–1323). In nine *Sermones* or *Autos-da-fé*[1] of the tribunal of Pamiers, condemning sixty-four persons, only five heretics were abandoned to the secular arm.

Bernard Gui presided over eighteen *autos-da-fé*, and condemned nine hundred and thirty heretics; and yet he abandoned only forty-two to the secular arm.[2] These Inquisitors were far more lenient than Robert the Bougre. Taking all in all, the Inquisition in its operation denoted a real progress in the treatment of criminals; for it not only put an end to the summary vengeance of the mob, but it diminished considerably the number of those sentenced to death.[3]

[1] The *Sermo generalis* after which the sentences were solemnly pronounced by the Inquisitors was called in Spain *auto-da-fé*.

[2] Cf. the sentences of Bernard Gui in Douais, *Documents*, vol. i, p. ccv, and Appendix B.

[3] Even while the Inquisition was in full operation, the heretics who managed to escape the ecclesiastical tribunals had no reason to congratulate themselves. For we read that Raymond VII, Count of Toulouse in 1248, caused eighty heretics to be burned at Berlaiges, near Agen, after they had confessed in his presence, without giving them the opportunity of recanting.

We notice at Pamiers that only one out of thirteen, while at Toulouse but one in twenty-two, was sentenced to death. Although terrible enough, these figures are far different from the exaggerated statistics imagined by the fertile brains of ignorant controversialists.[1]

It is true that many writers are haunted by the cruelty of the Spanish or German tribunals which sent to the stake a great number of victims, *i. e.*, *conversos* and witches.

From the very beginning, the Spanish Inquisition acted with the utmost severity. "Twelve hundred *conversos*, penitents, obdurate and relapsed heretics were present at the *auto-da-fé* in Toledo, March, 1487; and, according to the most conservative estimate, Torquemada sent to the stake about two thousand heretics"[2] in twelve years.

"During this same period," says a contemporary historian, "fifteen thousand heretics did penance, and were reconciled to the Church."[3] That makes a total

---

[1] Of course we do not here refer to honest historians like Langlois who estimates that one heretic out of every ten was abandoned to the secular arm (*op. cit.*, p. 106). Dom Brial erroneously states in his preface to vol. xix of the *Recueil des Historiens des Gaules* (p. xxiii) that Bernard Gui burned 637 heretics. This figure represented the number of heretics then known to be *condemned*, but only 40 of these were abandoned to the secular arm. The exact number is 42 out of 930. Cf. Douais, *Documents*, vol. i, p. ccv, and Appendix B.

[2] Langlois, *L'Inquisition d'après des tableaux récents*, 1902, pp. 105, 106. This number, without being certain, is asserted by contemporaries, Pulgar and Marineo Siculo. Cf. Héféle, *Le Cardinal Ximénes*, Paris, 1856, pp. 290, 291. Another contemporary, Bernaldes, speaks of over 700 burned from 1481-1488; cf. Gams, *Kirchengeschichte von Spanien*, vol. iii, 2, p. 69.

[3] Pulgar, in Héféle, *op. cit.*, p. 291.

of seventeen thousand trials. We can thus understand how Torquemada, although grossly calumniated, came to be identified with this period, during which so many thousands of *conversos* appeared before the Spanish tribunals.

The zeal of the Inquisitors seemed to abate after a time.[1] Perhaps they thought it better to keep the Jews and the Mussulmans in the Church by kindness. But kindness failed just as force had failed. After one hundred years, the number of obdurate *conversos* was as great as ever. Several ardent advocates of force advised the authorities to send them all to the stake. But the State determined to drive the Moriscos from Spain, as it had banished the Jews in 1492. Accordingly in September, 1609, a law was passed decreeing the banishment, under penalty of death, of all Moriscos, men, women, and children. Five hundred thousand persons, about one sixteenth of the population were thus banished from Spain, and forced to seek refuge on the coasts of Barbary. "Behold," writes Brother Bléda, "the most glorious event in Spain since the times of the Apostles; religious unity is now secured; an era of prosperity is certainly about to dawn."[2] This era of prosperity so proudly announced by the Dominican zealot never came. This extreme measure, which pleased him so greatly, in

[1] "The Inquisition of Valencia condemned one hundred and twelve *conversos* in 1538 (of whom fourteen were sent to the stake); at the *auto-da-fé* of Seville, September 24, 1559, three were burned, and eight were reconciled and sentenced to life imprisonment; on June 6, 1585, the Inquisitors of Saragossa in their account to Philip II speak of having reconciled sixty-three, and of having sent five to the stake." Langlois, *op. cit.*, p. 106.

[2] Cf. Bléda, *Defensio fidei in causa neophytorum sive Moriscorum regni Valentini totiusque Hispaniæ*, Valencia, 1610.

reality weakened Spain, by depriving her of hundreds of thousands of her subjects.

The witchcraft fever which spread over Europe in the fifteenth and sixteenth centuries stimulated to an extraordinary degree the zeal of the Inquisitors. The bull of Innocent VIII, *Summis Desiderantes*, December 5, 1484, made matters worse. The Pope admitted that men and women could have immoral relations with demons, and that sorcerers by their magical incantations could injure the harvests, the vineyards, the orchards and the fields.[1]

He also complained of the folly of those ecclesiastics and laymen who opposed the Inquisition in its prosecution of heretical sorcerers, and concluded by conferring additional powers upon the Dominican Inquisitors, Institoris and Sprenger, the author of the famous *Malleus Maleficarum*.

Innocent VIII assuredly had no intention of committing the Church to a belief in the phenomena he mentioned in his bull, but his personal opinion did have an influence upon the canonists and Inquisitors of his day; this is clear from the trials for witchcraft held during this period.[2] It is impossible to estimate the number of sorcerers condemned. Louis of Paramo triumphantly declared that in a century and a half the Holy Office sent to the stake over thirty thousand.[3] Of course we must take such round numbers with a grain of salt, as they always are greatly exaggerated.

[1] *Bullarium*, vol. v, p. 296 and seq., and Pegna's *Bullarium* in Eymeric, *Directorium Inquisit.*, p. 83.
[2] On this question, cf. Janssen-Pastor, *Geschichte des deutschen Volkes*, vol. viii, Fribourg, 1894, p. 507 and seq.
[3] *De Origine Officii sanctæ Inquisitionis*, p. 206.

But the fact remains that the condemnations for sorcery were so numerous as to stagger belief. The Papacy itself recognized the injustice of its agents. For in 1637 instructions were issued stigmatizing the conduct of the Inquisitors on account of their arbitrary and unjust prosecution of sorcerers; they were accused of extorting from them by cruel tortures confessions that were valueless, and of abandoning them to the secular arm without sufficient cause.[1]

. . . .

Confiscation, though not so severe a penalty as the stake, bore very heavily upon the victims of the Inquisition. The Roman laws classed the crime of heresy with treason, and visited it with a principal penalty, death, and a secondary penalty, confiscation. They decreed that all heretics, without exception, forfeited their property the very day they wavered in the faith. Actual confiscation of goods did not take place in the case of those penitents who had deserved no severer punishment than temporary imprisonment. Bernard Gui answered those who objected to this ruling, by showing that, as a matter of fact, there was no real pecuniary loss involved. For, he argued: " Secondary penances are inflicted only upon those heretics who denounce their accomplices. But, by this denunciation, they ensure the discovery and arrest of the guilty ones, who, without their aid, would have escaped punishment; the goods of these heretics are at once confiscated, which is certainly a positive gain." [2] Actual confiscation took place in the case of all obdurate

[1] Pignatelli, *Consultationes novissimæ canonicæ*, Venetiis, 2 in fol., vol. i, p. 505, *Consultatio* 123.
[2] *Practica*, 3 pars, p. 185.

and relapsed heretics abandoned to the secular arm, with all penitents condemned to perpetual imprisonment, and with all suspects who had managed to escape the Inquisition, either by flight or by death. The heretic who died peacefully in bed before the Inquisition could lay hands upon him was considered contumacious, and treated as such; his remains were exhumed, and his property confiscated. This last fact accounts for the incredible frequency of prosecutions against the dead. Of the six hundred and thirty-six cases tried by Bernard Gui, eighty-eight were posthumous. As a general rule, the confiscation of the heretic's property, which so frequently resulted from the trials of the Inquisition, had a great deal to do with the interest they aroused. We do not say that the Holy Office systematically increased the number of its condemnations merely to increase its pecuniary profits. But abuses of this kind were inevitable. We know they existed, because the Popes denounced them strongly, although they were too rare to deserve more than a passing mention. But would the ecclesiastical and lay princes who, in varying proportions, shared with the Holy Office in these confiscations, and who in some countries appropriated them all, have accorded to the Inquisition that continual good-will and help which was the condition of its prosperity, without what Lea calls "the stimulant of pillage?" We may very well doubt it. . . . That is why, in point of fact, their zeal for the faith languished whenever pecuniary gain was not forthcoming. "In our days," writes the Inquisitor Eymeric rather gloomily, "there are no more rich heretics, so that princes, not seeing much money in prospect, will not put themselves to any

THE INQUISITION

expense; it is a pity that so salutary an institution as ours should be so uncertain of its future." [1]

Most historians have said little or nothing about the money side of the Inquisition. Lea was the first to give it the attention it deserved. He writes: " In addition to the misery inflicted by these wholesale confiscations on the thousands of innocent and helpless women and children thus stripped of everything, it would be almost impossible to exaggerate the evil which they entailed upon all classes in the business of daily life." [2] There was indeed very little security in business, for the contracts of a hidden heretic were essentially null and void, and could be rescinded as soon as his guilt was discovered, either during his lifetime or after his death. In view of such a penal code, we can understand why Lea should write: "While the horrors of the crowded dungeon can scarce be exaggerated, yet more effective for evil and more widely exasperating was the sleepless watchfulness which was ever on the alert to plunder the rich and to wrench from the poor the hard-earned gains on which a family depended for support." [3]

. . . .

This summary of the acts of the Inquisition is at best but a brief and very imperfect outline. But a more complete study would not afford us any deeper insight into its operation.

Human passions are responsible for the many abuses of the Inquisition. The civil power in heresy trials

---

[1] Langlois, *op. cit.*, pp. 75–78.
[2] Lea, *op. cit.*, p. 522.
[3] Lea, *op. cit.*, p. 480.

was far from being partial to the accused. On the contrary, it would seem that the more pressure the State brought to bear upon the ecclesiastical tribunals, the more arbitrary their procedure became.

We do not deny that the zeal of the Inquisitors was at times excessive, especially in the use of torture. But some of their cruelty may be explained by their sincere desire for the salvation of the heretic. They regarded the confession of the suspects as the beginning of their conversion. They therefore believed any means used for that purpose justified. They thought that an Inquisitor had done something praiseworthy, when, even at the cost of cruel torments, he freed a heretic from his heresy. He was sorry indeed to be obliged to use force; but that was not altogether his fault, but the fault of the laws which he had to enforce.

Most men regard the *auto-da-fé* as the worst horror of the Inquisition. It is hardly ever pictured without burning flames and ferocious looking executioners. But an *auto-da-fé* did not necessarily call for either stake or executioner. It was simply a solemn "Sermon," which the heretics about to be condemned had to attend.[1] The death penalty was not always inflicted at these solemnities, which were intended to impress the imagination of the people. Seven out of eighteen *autos-da-fé* presided over by the famous Inquisitor, Bernard Gui, decreed no severer penalty than imprisonment.

We have seen, moreover, that in many places, even in Spain, at a certain period, the number of heretics condemned to death was rather small. Even Lea,

[1] On these " Sermons." cf. Tanon, *op., cit.* pp. 425–431.

THE INQUISITION

whom no one can accuse of any great partiality for the Church is forced to state: " The stake consumed comparatively few victims." [1]

In fact, imprisonment and confiscation were as a rule the severest penalties inflicted.

[1] *Op. cit.*, vol. i, p. 480.

CHAPTER X

A CRITICISM OF THE THEORY AND PRACTICE OF THE INQUISITION

SUCH was the development for over one thousand years (200–1300) of the theory of Catholic writers on the coercive power of the Church in the treatment of heresy. It began with the principle of absolute toleration; it ended with the stake.

During the era of the persecutions, the Church, who was suffering herself from pagan intolerance, merely excommunicated heretics, and tried to win them back to the orthodox faith by the kindness and the force of argument. But when the emperors became Christians, they, in memory of the days when they were "*Pontifices maximi*," at once endeavored to regulate worship and doctrine, at least externally. Unfortunately, certain sects, hated like the Manicheans, or revolutionary in character like the Donatists, prompted the enactment of cruel laws for their suppression. St. Optatus approved these measures, and Pope St. Leo had not the courage to disavow them. Still, most of the early Fathers, St. John Chrysostom, St. Martin, St. Ambrose, St. Augustine, and many others,[1]

---

[1] Lea (*op. cit.*, vol. i, pp. 214, 215) says that St. Jerome was an advocate of force. "Rigor in fact," argues St. Jerome, "is the most genuine mercy, since temporal punishment may avert eternal perdition." Here St. Jerome merely says that God punishes in time that He may not punish in eternity. But he

protested strongly in the name of Christian charity against the infliction of the death penalty upon heretics. St. Augustine, who formed the mind of his age, at first favored the theory of absolute toleration. But afterwards, perceiving that certain good results followed from what he called " a salutary fear," he modified his views. He then maintained that the State could and ought to punish by fine, confiscation, or even exile, her rebellious children, in order to make them repent. This may be called his theory of moderate persecution.

The revival of the Manichean heresy in the eleventh century took the Christian princes and people by surprise, unaccustomed as they were to the legislation of the first Christian emperors. Still the heretics did not fare any better on that account. For the people rose up against them, and burned them at the stake. The Bishops and the Fathers of the Church at once protested against this lynching of heretics. Some, like Wazo of Liège, represented the party of absolute toleration, while others, under the leadership of St. Bernard, advocated the theory of St. Augustine. Soon after, churchmen began to decree the penalty of imprisonment for heresy—a penalty unknown to the Roman law, and regarded in the beginning more as a penance than a legal punishment. It originated in the cloister, gradually made its way into the tribunals of the Bishop, and finally into the tribunals of the State.

Canon law, helped greatly by the revival of the imperial code, introduced in the twelfth century defi-

by no means " argues " that this punishment should be in the hands of either Church or State. *Commentar.*, in Naum, i, 9, P. L., vol. xxv, col. 1238

nite laws for the suppression of heresy. This régime lasted from 1150 till 1215, from Gratian to Innocent III. Heresy, the greatest sin against God, was classed with treason, and visited with the same penalty. The penalty was banishment with all its consequences; *i. e.*, the destruction of the houses of heretics, and the confiscation of their property. Still, because of the horror which the Church had always professed for the effusion of blood, she did not as yet inflict the death penalty which the State decreed for treason. Innocent III did not wish to go beyond the limits set by St. Augustine, St. John Chrysostom, and St. Bernard.

But later Popes and princes went further. They began by decreeing death as a secondary penalty, in case heretics rebelled against the law of banishment. But when the Emperor Frederic had revived the legislation of his Christian predecessors of the fourth, fifth, and sixth centuries,[1] and had made the popular custom of burning heretics a law of the empire, the Papacy could not resist the current of his example. The Popes at once ordered the new legislation vigorously enforced everywhere, especially in Lombardy. This was simply the logical carrying out of the comparison made by Innocent III between heresy and treason, and was due chiefly to two Popes: Gregory IX who established the Inquisition under the Dominicans and the Franciscans, and Innocent IV who authorized the Inquisitors to use torture.

The theologians and casuists soon began to defend the procedure of the Inquisition. They seemed absolutely unaffected, in theory at least, by the most cruel torments. With them the preservation of the

[1] Cf. the law of Arcadius of 395 (*Cod. Theodos.*, xvi, v. 28).

orthodox faith was paramount, and superior to all sentiment. In the name of Christian charity, St. Thomas, the great light of the thirteenth century, taught that relapsed heretics, even when repentant, ought to be put to death without mercy.

How are we to explain this development of the doctrine of the Church on the suppression of heresy, and granting that a plausible explanation may be given, how are we to justify it?

. . . .

Intolerance is natural to man. If, as a matter of fact, men are not always intolerant in practice, it is only because they are prevented by conditions born of reason and wisdom. Respect for the opinion of others supposes a temper of mind which takes years to acquire. It is a question whether the average man is capable of it. Intolerance regarding religious doctrines especially, with the cruelty that usually accompanies it, has practically been the law of history. From this viewpoint, the temper of mind of the mediæval Christians differed little from that of the pagans of the empire. A Roman of the second or third century considered blasphemy against the gods a crime that deserved the greatest torments; a Christian of the eleventh century felt the same toward the apostates and enemies of the Catholic faith. This is clearly seen from the treatment accorded the first Manicheans who came from Bulgaria, and gained some adherents at Orléans, Montwimer, Soissons, Liège, and Goslar. At once there was a popular uprising against them, which evidenced what may be called the instinctive intolerance of the people. The civil authorities of the day shared this hatred, and proved it either by sending heretics to the stake themselves, or allowing the people to do so. As Lea has said: " The practice of burning the heretic alive was thus not the creation of positive law, but arose generally and spontaneously, and its adoption by the legislator was only the recognition of a popular custom." [1] Besides, the sovereign could not brook riotous men who disturbed the established order of his dominions. He was well aware that public tranquillity depended chiefly upon religious principles, which ensured that moral unity desired by every ruler. Pagan antiquity had dreamed of this unity, and its philosophers, interpreting its mind, showed themselves just as intolerant as the theologians of the Middle Ages.

" Plato," writes Gaston Boissier, " in his ideal *Republic*, denies toleration to the impious, *i. e.*, to those who did not accept the State religion. Even if they remained quiet and peaceful, and carried on no propaganda, they seemed to him dangerous by the bad example they gave. He condemned them to be shut up in a house where they might learn wisdom (*sophronisteria*)—by this pleasant euphemism he meant a prison—and for five years they were to listen to a discourse every day. The impious who caused disturbance and tried to corrupt others were to be imprisoned for life in a terrible dungeon, and after death were to be denied burial." [2] Apart from the stake, was not this the Inquisition to the life? In countries where religion and patriotism went hand in hand, we can readily conceive this intolerance. Sovereigns were

[1] Lea, *op. cit.*, vol. i, p. 222.
[2] *La fin du paganisme*, vol. i, pp. 47, 48. Cf. Plato's *Republic*, Book II; Laws, Book X.

THE INQUISITION

naturally inclined to believe that those who interfered with the public worship unsettled the State, and their conviction became all the stronger when the State received from heaven a sort of special investiture. This was the case with the Christian empire. Constantine, towards the end of his career, thought himself ordained by God, " a bishop in externals," [1] and his successors strove to keep intact the deposit of faith. " The first care of the imperial majesty," said one of them, " is to protect the true religion, for with its worship is connected the prosperity of human undertakings."[2] Thus some of their laws were passed in view of strengthening the canon law. They mounted guard about the Church, with sword in hand, ready to use it in her defence.

The Middle Ages inherited these views. Religious unity was then attained throughout Europe. Any attempt to break it was an attack at once upon the Church and the Empire. " The enemies of the Cross of Christ and those who deny the Christian faith," says Pedro II, of Aragon, " are also our enemies, and the public enemies of our kingdom; they must be treated as such."[3] It was in virtue of the same principle that Frederic II punished heretics as criminals according to the common law; *ut crimina publica.* He speaks of the " Ecclesiastical peace " as of old the emperors spoke of the " Roman peace." As Emperor, he considered it his duty " to preserve and to maintain it," and woe betide the one who dared disturb it. Feeling himself invested with both human

---

[1] Eusebius, *Vita Constantini*, lib. iv, cap. xxiv.
[2] Theodosius II, *Novellæ*, tit. iii (438).
[3] Law of 1197, in De Marca, *Marca Hispanica*, col. 1384.

and divine authority, he enacted the severest laws possible against heresy. What therefore might have remained merely a threatening theory became a terrible reality. The laws of 1224, 1231, 1238, and 1239 prove that both princes and people considered the stake a fitting penalty for heresy.

It would have been very surprising if the Church menaced as she was by an ever-increasing flood of heresy, had not accepted the State's eager offer of protection. She had always professed a horror for bloodshed. But as long as she was not acting directly, and the State undertook to shed in its own name the blood of wicked men, she began to consider solely the benefits that would accrue to her from the enforcement of the civil laws. Besides, by classing heresy with treason, she herself had laid down the premises of the State's logical conclusion, the death penalty. The Church, therefore, could hardly call in question the justice of the imperial laws, without in a measure going against the principles she herself had advocated.

Church and State, therefore, continually influenced one the other. The theory upheld by the Church reacted on the State and caused it to adopt violent measures, while the State in turn compelled the Church to approve its use of force, although such an attitude was opposed to the spirit of early Christianity.

The theologians and the canonists put the finishing touches to the situation. Influenced by what was happening around them, their one aim was to defend the laws of their day. This is clearly seen, if we compare the *Summa* of St. Raymond of Pennafort with the *Summa* of St. Thomas Aquinas. When St. Raymond wrote his work, the Church still followed the criminal code of Popes Lucius III and Innocent III; she had as yet no notion of inflicting the death penalty for heresy. But in St. Thomas's time, the Inquisition had been enforcing for some years the draconian laws of Frederic II. The Angelic Doctor, therefore, made no attempt to defend the obsolete code of Innocent III, but endeavored to show that the imperial laws, then authorized by the Church, were comformable to the strictest justice. His one argument was to make comparisons, more or less happy, between heresy and crimes against the common law.

At a period when no one considered a doctrine solidly proved unless authorities could be quoted in its support, these comparisons were not enough. So the theologians taxed their ingenuity to find quotations, not from the Fathers, which would have been difficult, but from the Scriptures, which seemed favorable to the ideas then in vogue. St. Optatus had tried to do this as early as the fifth century,[1] despite the antecedent protests of Origen, Cyprian, Lactantius and Hilary. Following his example, the churchmen of the Middle Ages reminded their hearers that according to the Sacred Scriptures, "Jehovah was a God delighting in the extermination of his enemies." They read how Saul, the chosen king of Israel, had been divinely punished for sparing Agag of Amalek; how the prophet Samuel had hewn him to pieces; how the wholesale slaughter of the unbelieving Canaanites had been ruthlessly commanded and enforced; how Elijah had been commended for slaying four hundred and fifty priests of Baal; and they could not conceive how mercy to those who rejected the true faith could be aught but

[1] *De Schismate Donatistarum*, p. iii, cap. vii.

disobedience to God. Had not Almighty God said: "If thy brother, the son of thy mother, or thy daughter or thy wife, that is in thy bosom, or thy friend, whom thou lovest as thy own soul, would persuade thee secretly, saying: 'Let us go and serve strange gods,' which thou knowest not, nor thy fathers . . . consent not to him, hear him not, neither let thy eye spare him to pity or conceal him, but thou shalt presently put him to death. Let thy hand be first upon him, and afterwards the hands of all the people." [1]

Such a teaching might appear, at first sight, hard to reconcile with the law of gentleness which Jesus preached to the world. But the theologians quoted Christ's words: "Do not think that I am come to destroy the law; I am not come to destroy but to fulfill," [2] and other texts of the Gospels to prove the perfect agreement between the Old and the New Law in the matter of penalties. They even went so far as to assert that St. John [3] spoke of the penalty of fire to be inflicted upon heretics.

This strange method of exegesis was not peculiar to the founders and the defenders of the tribunals of the Inquisition. England, which knew nothing of the Inquisition, save for the trial of the Templars, was just as cruel to heretics as Gregory IX or Frederic II.

"The statute of May 25, 1382, directs the king to issue to his sheriffs commissions to arrest Wyclif's traveling preachers, and aiders and abettors of heresy, and hold them till they justify themselves *selon reson et la ley de seinte esglise*. After the burning of Sawtré

---

[1] Deut. xiii. 6–9; cf. xvii. 1–6.
[2] Matt. v. 17.
[3] John xv. 16.

by a royal warrant confirmed by Parliament in 1400, the statute '*de hæreticis comburendis*' for the first time inflicted in England the death penalty as a settled punishment for heresy. . . . It forbade the dissemination of heretical opinions and books, empowered the bishops to seize all offenders and hold them in prison until they should purge themselves or abjure, and ordered the bishops to proceed against them within three months after arrest. For minor offences, the bishops were empowered to imprison during pleasure and fine at discretion,—the fine enuring to the royal exchequer. For obstinate heresy or relapse, involving under the canon law abandonment to the secular arm, the bishops and their commissioners were the sole judges, and on their delivery of such convicts, the sheriff of the county, or the mayor and bailiffs of the nearest town, were obliged to burn them before the people on an eminence. Henry V followed this up, and the statute of 1414 established throughout the kingdom a sort of mixed secular and ecclesiastical Inquisition for which the English system of grand inquests gave special facilities. Under this legislation, burning for heresy became a not unfamiliar sight for English eyes, and Lollardy was readily suppressed. In 1533, Henry VIII repealed the statute of 1400, while retaining those of 1382 and 1414, and also the penalty of burning alive for contumacious heresy and relapse, and the dangerous admixture of politics and religion rendered the stake a favorite instrument of statecraft. One of the earliest measures of the reign of Edward VI was the repeal of this law, as well as those of 1382 and 1414, together with all the atrocious legislation of the Six Articles. With the reaction under

Philip and Mary, came a revival of the sharp laws against heresy. Scarce had the Spanish marriage been concluded when an obedient Parliament re-enacted the legislation of 1382, 1400, and 1414, which afforded ample machinery for the numerous burnings which followed. The earliest act of the first Parliament of Elizabeth was the repeal of the legislation of Philip and Mary, and of the old statutes which it had revived; but the writ *de hæretico comburendo* had become an integral part of English law, and survived, until the desire of Charles II for Catholic toleration caused him, in 1676, to procure its abrogation, and the restraint of the ecclesiastical courts in cases of atheism, blasphemy, heresy, and schism, and other damnable doctrines and opinions ' to the ecclesiastical remedies of excommunication, deprivation, degradation, and other ecclesiastical censures, not extending to death." [1]

These ideas of intolerance were so fixed in the public mind at the close of the Middle Ages, that even those who protested against the procedure of the Inquisition thought that in principle it was just. Farel wrote to Calvin, September 8, 1533: "Some people do not wish us to prosecute heretics. But because the Pope condemns the faithful (*i. e.*, the Huguenots) for the crime of heresy, and because unjust judges punish the innocent, it is absurd to conclude that we must not put heretics to death, in order to strengthen the faithful. I myself have often said that I was ready to suffer death, if I ever taught anything contrary to sound doctrine, and that I would deserve the most frightful torments, if I tried to rob any one of the true faith in

---

[1] Lea, *op. cit.*, vol. i, pp. 352-354.

Christ. I cannot, therefore, lay down a different law to others." [1]

Calvin held the same views. His inquisitorial spirit was manifest in his bitter prosecution and condemnation of the Spaniard Michael Servetus.[2] When any one found fault with him he answered: " The executioners of the Pope taught that their foolish inventions were doctrines of Christ, and were excessively cruel, while I have always judged heretics in all kindness and in the fear of God; I merely put to death a confessed heretic." [3] Michael Servetus assuredly did not gain much by the substitution of Calvin for the Inquisition.

Bullinger of Zurich, speaking of the death of Servetus, thus wrote Lelius Socinus: " If, Lelius, you cannot now admit the right of a magistrate to punish heretics, you will undoubtedly admit it some day. St Augustine himself at first deemed it wicked to use violence towards heretics, and tried to win them back by the mere word of God. But finally, learning wisdom by experience, he began to use force with good effect. In the beginning the Lutherans did not believe that heretics ought to be punished; but after the

[1] *Œuvres complètes de Calvin*, Brunswick, 1863–1900, vol. xiv, p. 612.

[2] Servetus was condemned October 26, 1553, to be burned alive, and was executed the next day. As early as 1545, Calvin had written: " If he (Servetus) comes to Geneva, I will never allow him to depart alive, as long as I have authority in this city: *Vivum exire numquam patiar*. *Œuvres complètes*, vol. xii, p. 283." Calvin, however, wished the death penalty of fire to be commuted into some other kind of death.

[3] To justify this execution, Calvin published his *Defensio orthodoxœ fidei de sacra Trinitate, contra prodigiosos errores Michælis Serveti Hispani, ubi ostenditur hæreticos jure gladii cœrcendos esse*. Geneva, 1554.

excesses of the Anabaptists, they declared that the magistrate ought not merely to reprimand the unruly, but to punish them severely as an example to thousands."

Theodore of Beza, who had seen several of his coreligionists burned in France for their faith, likewise wrote in 1554, in Calvinistic Geneva: "What crime can be greater or more heinous than heresy, which sets at nought the word of God and all ecclesiastic discipline? Christian magistrates, do your duty to God, Who has put the sword into your hands for the honor of His majesty; strike valiantly these monsters in the guise of men." Theodore of Beza considered the error of those who demanded freedom of conscience " worse than the tyranny of the Pope. It is better to have a tyrant, no matter how cruel he may be, than to let everyone do as he pleases." He maintained that the sword of the civil authority should punish not only heretics, but also those who wished heresy to go unpunished.[1] In brief, before the Renaissance there were very few who taught with Huss[2] that a heretic ought not to be abandoned to the secular arm to be put to death.[3]

---

[1] *De hæreticis a civili magistratu puniendis*, Geneva, 1554; translated into French by Colladon in 1559.

[2] In his treatise *De Ecclesia*. This was the eighteenth article of the heresies attributed to him.

[3] In general, the Protestant leaders of the day were glad of the execution of Servetus. Melancthon wrote to Bullinger: " I am astonished that some persons denounce the severity that was so justly used in that case." Among those who did denounce it was Nicolas Zurkinden of Berne. Cf. his letter in the *Œuvres complètes de Calvin*, vol. xv, p. 19. Sébastien Castellio published in March, 1554, his *Traité des hérétiques, a savoir s'il faut les persécuter*, the oldest and one of the most eloquent pamphlets

Such severity, nay, such cruelty, shown to what we would call " a crime of opinion," is hard for men of our day to understand. "To comprehend it," says Lea, " we must picture to ourselves a stage of civilization in many respects wholly unlike our own. Passions were fiercer, convictions stronger, virtues and vices more exaggerated, than in our colder and self-contained time. The age, moreover, was a cruel one. . . . We have only to look upon the atrocities of the criminal law of the Middle Ages to see how pitiless men were in their dealings with one another. The wheel, the caldron of burning oil, burning alive, tearing apart with wild horses, were the ordinary expedients by which the criminal jurist sought to deter men from crime by frightful examples which would make a profound impression on a not over-sensitive population." [1]

When we consider this rigorous civil criminal code, we need not wonder that heretics, who were considered the worst possible criminals, were sent to the stake.

This explains why intelligent men, animated by the purest zeal for good, proved so hard and unbending, and used without mercy the most cruel tortures, when they thought that the faith or the salvation of souls was at stake. "With such men," says Lea,—and he mentions among others Innocent III and St. Louis,— " it was not hope of gain, or lust of blood or pride of

against intolerance. Cf. F. Buisson, *op. cit.*, ch. xi. This is the pamphlet that Theodore of Beza tried to refute. Castellio then attacked Calvin directly in a new work, *Contra libellum Calvini in quo ostendere conatur hæreticos jure gladii cœrcendos esse*, which was not published until 1612, in Holland.

[1] Lea, *op. cit.*, vol. i, pp. 234, 235.

opinion, or wanton exercise of power, but sense of duty, and they but represented what was universal public opinion from the thirteenth to the seventeenth centuries."

It was, therefore, the spirit of the times, the *Zeitgeist*, as we would call it to-day, that was responsible for the rigorous measures formerly used by both Church and State in the suppression of heresy. The other reasons we have mentioned are only subsidiary. This is the one reason that satisfactorily explains both the theories and the facts.

But an explanation is something far different from a defence of an institution. To explain is to show the relation of cause to effect; to defend is to show that the effect corresponds to an ideal of justice. Even if we grant that the procedure of the Inquisition did correspond to a certain ideal of justice, that ideal is certainly not ours to-day. Let us go into this question more thoroughly.

It is obvious that we must strongly denounce all the abuses of the Inquisition that were due to the sins of individuals, no matter what their source. No one, for instance, would dream of defending Cauchon, the iniquitous judge of Joan of Arc, or other cruel Inquisitors who, like him, used their authority to punish unjustly suspects brought before their tribunal. From this standpoint, it is probable that many of the sentences of the Inquisition need revision.

But can we rightly consider this institution " a sublime spectacle of social perfection," and " a model of justice ? "[2]

[1] Lea, *op. cit.*, vol. i, p. 234.
[2] The *Civiltà Cattolica*, 1853, vol. i, p. 595 seq.

To call the Inquisition a model of justice is a manifest exaggeration, as every fair student of its history must admit.

The Inquisitorial procedure was, in itself, inferior to the *accusatio*, in which the accuser assumed the burden of publicly proving his charges. That it was difficult to observe this method of procedure in heresy trials can readily be understood; for the *pœna talionis* awaiting the accuser who failed to substantiate his charges was calculated to cool the ardor of many Catholics, who otherwise would have been eager to prosecute heretics. But we must grant that the *accusatio* in criminal law allowed a greater chance for justice to be done than the *inquisitio*. Besides, if the ecclesiastical *inquisitio* had proceeded like the civil *inquisitio*, the possibility of judicial errors might have been far less. "In the *inquisitio* of the civil law, the secrecy for for which the Inquisition has been justly criticized, did not exist; the suspect was cited, and a copy of the *capitula* or *articuli* containing the charges was given to him. When questioned, he could either confess or deny these charges. The names of the witnesses who were to appear against him, and a copy of their testimony, were also supplied, so that he could carry on his defence either by objecting to the character of his accusers, or the tenor of their charges. Women, minors aged fourteen, serfs, enemies of the prisoner, criminals, excommunicates, heretics, and those branded with infamy were not allowed to testify. All testimony was received in writing. The prisoner and his lawyers then appeared before the judge to rebut the evidence and the charges."[1]

[1] Tanon, *op. cit.*, pp. 287, 288.

In the ecclesiastical procedure, on the contrary, the names of the witnesses were withheld, save in very exceptional cases; any one could testify, even if he were a heretic; the prisoner had the right to reject all whom he considerd his mortal enemies, but even then he had to guess at their names in order to invalidate their testimony; he was not allowed a lawyer, but had to defend himself in secret. Only the most prejudiced minds can consider such a procedure the ideal of justice. On the contrary, it is unjust in every detail wherein it differs from the *inquisitio* of the civil law.

Certain reasons may be adduced to explain the attitude of the Popes, who wished to make the procedure of the Inquisition as secret and as comprehensive as possible. They were well aware of the danger that witnesses would incur, if their names were indiscreetly revealed. They knew that the publicity of the pleadings would certainly hinder the efficiency of heresy trials. But such considerations do not change the character of the institution itself; the Inquisition in leaving too great a margin to the arbitrary conduct of individual judges, at once fell below the standard of strict justice.

All that can and ought to be said in the defence and to the honor of the Roman pontiffs is that they endeavored to remedy the abuses of the Inquisition. With this in view, Innocent IV and Alexander IV obliged the Inquisitors to consult a number of *boni viri* and *periti;* Clement V forbade them to render any grave decision without first consulting the bishops, the natural judges of the faith;[1] and Boniface VIII

---

[1] Clementinæ, *De Hæreticis*, Decretal *Multorum Querela*, cap i, sect. i.

THE INQUISITION 169

recommended them to reveal the names of the witnesses to the prisoners, if they thought that this revelation would not be prejudicial to any one.[1] In a word, they wished the laws of justice to be scrupulously observed, and at times mitigated.[2] But, examined in detail, these laws were far from being perfect.

. . . .

Antecedent imprisonment and torture, which played so important a part in the procedure of the Inquisition, were undoubtedly very barbarous methods of judicial prosecution. Antecedent imprisonment may be justified in certain cases; but the manner in which the Inquisitors conceived it was far from just. No one would dare defend to-day the punishment known as the *carcer durus*, whereby the Inquisitors tried to extort confessions from their prisoners. They rendered it, moreover, all the more odious by arbitrarily prolonging its horrors and its cruelty.

It is harder still to reconcile the use of torture with any idea of justice. If the Inquisitors had stopped at flogging, which according to St. Augustine was administered at home, in school, and even in the episcopal tribunals of the early ages, and is mentioned by the Council of Agde, in 506, and the Benedictine rule, no one would have been greatly scandalized. We might perhaps have considered this domestic and paternal custom a little severe, but perfectly consistent with the

[1] Sexto, *De Hæreticis*, cap. xx; cf. Tanon, *op. cit.*, p. 391.
[2] Döllinger is very unjust when he says: "From 1200 to 1500 there is a long uninterrupted series of papal decrees on the Inquisition; these decrees increase continually in severity and cruelty." *La Papauté*, p. 102. Tanon (*op. cit.*, p. 138) writes more impartially: "Clement V, instead of increasing the powers of the Holy Office, tried rather to suppress its abuses."

ideas men then had of goodness. But the rack, the *strappado*, and the stake were peculiarly inhuman inventions.[1] When the pagans used them against the Christians of the first centuries, all agreed in stigmatizing them as the extreme of barbarism, or as inventions of the devil. Their character did not change when the Inquisition began to use them against heretics. To our shame we are forced to admit that, notwithstanding Innocent IV's appeal for moderation,[2] the brutality of the ecclesiastical tribunals was often on a par with the tribunals of the pagan persecutors. Pope Nicholas I thus denounced the use of torture as a means of judical inquiry: "Such proceedings," he says, "are contrary to the law of God and of man, for a confession ought to be spontaneous, not forced; it ought to be free, and not the result of violence. A prisoner may endure all the torments you inflict upon him without confessing anything. Is not that a disgrace to the judge, and an evident proof of his inhumanity! If, on the contrary, a prisoner, under stress of torture, acknowledges himself guilty of a crime he never committed, is not the one who forced him to lie, guilty of a heinous crime?"[3]

. . . .

The penalties which the tribunals of the Inquisition inflicted upon heretics are harder to judge. Let us observe, first of all, that the majority of the heretics abandoned to the secular arm merited the most severe

[1] This was the view of St. Augustine, *Ep.* cxxxiii, 2.

[2] Bull *Ad Extirpanda*, in Eymeric, *Directorium inquisitorum*, Appendix, p. 8.

[3] *Responsa ad consulta Bulgarorum*, cap. lxxxvi; Labbe, *Concilia*, vol. viii, col. 544.

punishment for their crimes. It would surely have been unjust for criminals against the common law to escape punishment under cover of their religious belief. Crimes committed in the name of religion are always crimes, and the man who has his property stolen or is assaulted cares little whether he has to deal with a religious fanatic or an ordinary criminal. In such instances, the State is not defending a particular dogmatic teaching, but her own most vital interests. Heretics, therefore, who were criminals against the civil law were justly punished. An anti-social sect like the Cathari, which shrouded itself in mystery and perverted the people so generally, by the very fact of its existence and propaganda called for the vengeance of society and the sword of the State.

"However much," says Lea, "we may deprecate the means used for its suppression, and commiserate those who suffered for conscience' sake, we cannot but admit that the cause of orthodoxy was in this case the cause of progress and civilization. Had Catharism become dominant, or even had it been allowed to exist on equal terms, its influence could not have failed to prove disastrous. Its asceticism with regard to commerce between the sexes, if strictly enforced, could only have led to the extinction of the race. . . . Its condemnation of the visible universe, and of matter in general as the work of Satan rendered sinful all striving after material improvement, and the conscientious belief in such a creed could only lead man back, in time, to his original condition of savagism. It was not only a revolt against the Church, but a renunciation of man's domination over nature."[1] Its growth

[1] Lea, *op. cit.*, vol. i, p. 106.

had to be arrested at any price. Society, in prosecuting it without mercy, was only defending herself against the working of an essentially destructive force. It was a struggle for existence.

We must, therefore, deduct from the number of those who are commonly styled the victims of ecclesiastical intolerance, the majority of the heretics executed by the State; for nearly all that were imprisoned or sent to the stake, especially in northern Italy and southern France, were Cathari.[1]

This important observation has so impressed certain historians, that they have been led to think the Inquisition dealt only with criminals of this sort. " History," says Rodrigo, " has preserved the record of the outrages committed by the heretics of Bulgaria, the Gnostics, and the Manicheans; the death sentence was inflicted only upon criminals who confessed their murders, robberies, and acts of violence. The Albigenses were treated with kindness. The Catholic Church deplores all acts of vengeance, however strong the provocation given by these factious mobs." [2]

Such a defence of the Inquisition is not borne out by the facts. It is true, of course, that in the Middle Ages there was hardly a heresy which had not some connection with an anti-social sect. For this reason any one who denied a dogma of the faith was at once suspected, rightly or wrongly, of being an anarchist. But,

[1] Jean Guiraud has proved that the Waldenses, Fraticelli, Hussites, Lollards, etc., attacked society, which acted in self-defence when she put them to death. *La répression de l'hérésie au moyen âge*, in the *Questions d'histoire et d'archéologie Chrétienne*, p. 24 and seq.

[2] *Historia verdadera de la Inquisicion*, Madrid, 1876, vol. i, pp. 176, 177.

THE INQUISITION

as a matter of fact, the Inquisition did not condemn merely those heresies which caused social upheaval, but all heresies are such: "We decree," says Frederic II, " that the crime of heresy, no matter what the name of the sect, be classed as a public crime. . . and that every one who denies the Catholic faith, even in one article, shall be liable to the law: *si inventi fuerint a fide catholica saltem in articulo deviare.*" [1] This was also the view of the theologians and the canonists. St. Thomas Aquinas, for instance, who speaks for the whole *schola*, did not make any distinction between the Catharan heresy and any other purely speculative heresy; he put them all on one level; every obdurate or relapsed heretic deserved death.[2] The Inquisitors were so fully persuaded of this truth that they prosecuted heretics whose heresy was not discovered until ten or twenty years after their death, when surely they were no longer able to cause any injury to society.[3]

We need not wonder at these views and practices, for they were fully in accord with the notion of justice current at the time. The rulers in Church and State felt it their duty not only to defend the social order, but to safeguard the interests of God in the world. They deemed themselves in all sincerity the representatives of divine authority here below. God's interests were their interests; it was their duty, therefore, to punish all crimes against His law. Heresy, therefore, a purely theological crime, became amenable to their tribunal. In punishing it, they believed that they were merely fulfilling one of the duties of their

---

[1] Constitution *Inconsutilem tunicam.*
[2] *Summa* IIa, IIae, q. x, art. 8; q. xi, art. 3 and 4.
[3] Cf. Tanon, *op. cit.*, pp. 407–412.

office. We have now to examine and judge the penalties inflicted upon heresy as such.

The first in order of importance was the death penalty of the stake, inflicted upon all obdurate and relapsed heretics.

Relapsed heretics, when repentant, did not at first incur the death penalty. Imprisonment was considered an adequate punishment, for it gave them a chance to expiate their fault. The death penalty inflicted later on placed the judges in a false position. On the one hand, by granting absolution and giving communion to the prisoner, they professed to believe in the sincerity of his repentance and conversion, and yet by sending him to the stake for fear of a relapse, they acted contrary to their convictions. To condemn a man to death who was considered worthy of receiving the Holy Eucharist, on the plea that he might one day commit the sin of heresy again, appears to us a crying injustice.

But should even unrepentant heretics be put to death? No, taught St. Augustine, and most of the early Fathers, who invoked in favor of the guilty ones the higher law of " charity and Christian gentleness." Their doctrine certainly accorded perfectly with our Saviour's teaching, in the parable of the cockle and the good grain. As Wazo, Bishop of Liège said: " May not those who are to-day cockle become wheat to-morrow?"[1] But in decreeing the death of these sinners, the Inquisitors at once did away with the possibility of their conversion. Certainly this was not in accordance with Christian charity. Such severity can only be defended by the authority of the Old Law, whose

[1] *Vita Vasonis*, cap. xxv, in Migne, P. L., vol. cxlii, col. 753.

severity, according to the early Fathers, had been abolished by the law of Christ.[1]

Advocates of the death penalty, like Frederic II and St. Thomas, tried to defend their view by arguments from reason. Criminals guilty of treason, and counterfeiters are condemned to death. Therefore, heretics who are traitors and falsifiers merit the same penalty. But a comparison of this kind is not necessarily a valid argument. The criminals in question were a grave menace to the social order. But we cannot say as much for each and every heresy in itself. It was unjust to place a crime against society and a sin against God on an equal footing. Such reasoning would prove that all sins were crimes of treason against God, and therefore merited death.[2] Is not a sacrilegious communion the worst possible insult to the divine majesty? Must we argue, therefore, that every unworthy communicant, if unrepentant, must be sent to the stake?

It is evident, therefore, that neither reason, Christian tradition nor the New Testament call for the infliction

---

[1] St. Optatus (*De Schismate Donatistarum*, lib. iii, cap. vi and vii) was one of the first of the Fathers to quote the Old Testament as his authority for the infliction of the death penalty upon heretics. But in this he was not followed either by his contemporaries or his immediate successors. Before him, Origen and St. Cyprian had protested against this appeal to the Mosaic law.

[2] Mgr. Bonomelli, Bishop of Cremona, writes: "In the Middle Ages, they reasoned thus: If rebellion against the prince deserves death, *a fortiori* does rebellion against God. Singular logic! It is not very hard to put one's finger upon the utter absurdity of such reasoning. For every sinner is a rebel against God's law. It follows then that we ought to condemn all men to death, beginning with the kings and the legislators;" quoted by Morlais in the *Revue du Clergé Français*, August 1, 1905, p. 457.

of the death penalty upon heretics. The interpretation of St. John xv. 6: *Si quis in me non manserit, in ignem mittent et ardet*, made by the mediæval canonists, is not worth discussing. It was an abuse of the accommodated sense which bordered on the ridiculous, although its consequences were terrible.

. . . .

Modern apologists have clearly recognized this. For that reason they have tried their best to show that the execution of heretics was solely the work of the civil power, and that the Church was in no way responsible.

"When we argue about the Inquisition," says Joseph de Maistre, "let us separate and distinguish very carefully the rôle of the Church and the rôle of the State. All that is terrible and cruel about this tribunal, especially its death penalty, is due to the State; that was its business, and it alone must be held to an accounting. All the clemency, on the contrary, which plays so large a part in the tribunal of the Inquisition must be ascribed to the Church, which interfered in its punishments only to suppress and mitigate them."[1] "The Church," says another grave historian, "took no part in the corporal punishment of heretics. Those executed were simply punished for their crimes, and were condemned by judges acting under the royal seal."[2] "This," says Lea, "is a typical instance in which history is written to order. . . . It is altogether a modern perversion of history to assume, as apologists do, that the request for mercy was sincere, and that

[1] *Lettres à un gentilhomme russe sur l'Inquisition espagnole*, ed. 1864, pp. 17, 18, 28, 34.

[2] Rodrigo, *Historia verdadera de la Inquisicion*, 1876, vol. i, p. 176.

the secular magistrate and not the Inquisition was responsible for the death of the heretic. We can imagine the smile of amused surprise with which Gregory IX and Gregory XI would have listened to the dialectics with which Count Joseph de Maistre proves that it is an error to suppose, and much more to assert, that a Catholic priest can in any manner be instrumental in compassing the death of a fellow creature." [1]

The real share of the Inquisition in a condemnation involving the death penalty is indeed a very difficult question to determine. According to the letter of the papal and imperial Constitutions of 1231 and 1232, the civil and not the ecclesiastical tribunals assumed all responsibility for the death sentence;[2] the Inquisition merely decided upon the question of doctrine, leaving the rest to the secular Court. It is this legislation that the above-named apologists have in mind, and the text of these laws is on their side.

But when we consider how these laws were carried out in practice, we must admit that the Church did have some share in the death sentence. We have already seen that the Church excommunicated those princes who refused to burn the heretics which the Inquisition handed over to them. The princes were not really judges in this case; the right to consider questions of heresy was formally denied them.[3] It was their duty simply to register the decree of the Church, and to enforce it according to the civil law. In every execution, therefore, a twofold authority

[1] Lea, *op. cit.*, vol. i, pp. 540, 227.
[2] Decretals, cap. xv, *De Hæreticis*, lib. v, tit. vii. *Mon. Germ., Leges*, sect. iv, vol. ii, p. 196.
[3] Cf. Sexto, v, ii, cap. xi, and xviii. *De Hæreticis*, in Eymeric, *Directorum*, p. 110.

came into play: the civil power which carried out its own laws, and the spiritual power which forced the State to carry them out. That is why Peter Cantor declared that the Cathari ought not to be put to death after an ecclesiastical trial, lest the Church be compromised: "*Illud ab eo fit, cujus auctoritate fit,*" he said, to justify his recommendation.[1]

It is therefore erroneous to pretend that the Church had absolutely no part in the condemnation of heretics to death. It is true that this participation of hers was not direct and immediate; but, even though indirect, it was none the less real and efficacious.[2]

The judges of the Inquisition realized this, and did their best to free themselves of this responsibility which weighed rather heavily upon them. Some maintained that in compelling the civil authority to enforce the existing laws, they were not going outside their spiritual office, but were merely deciding a case of conscience. But this theory was unsatisfactory. To reassure their consciences, they tried another expedient. In abandoning heretics to the secular arm, they besought the state officials to act with moderation, and avoid " all bloodshed and all danger of death." This was unfortunately an empty formula which deceived no one. It was intended to safeguard the principle which the Church had taken for her motto: *Ecclesia abhorret a*

[1] *Verbum abbreviatum*, cap. lxxviii, P. L., vol. ccv, col. 231.

[2] In Spain, the manner in which the Inquisition abandoned heretics to the secular arm denoted a real participation of the State in the execution of heretics. The evening before the execution the Inquisitors brought the King a small fagot tied with ribbons. The King at once requested " that this fagot be the first thrown upon the fire in his name." Cf. Baudrillart, *A propos de l'Inquisition*, in the *Revue Pratique d'Apologétique*, July 15, 1906, p. 354, note.

sanguine. In strongly asserting this traditional law, the Inquisitors imagined that they thereby freed themselves from all responsibility, and kept from imbruing their hands in bloodshed. We must take this for what it is worth. It has been styled "cunning" and "hypocrisy;"[1] let us call it simply a legal fiction.

. . . .

The penalty of life imprisonment and the penalty of confiscation inflicted upon so many heretics, was like the death penalty imposed only by the secular arm. We must add to this banishment, which was inscribed in the imperial legislation, and reappeared in the criminal codes of Lucius III and Innocent III. These several penalties were by their nature vindicative. For this reason they were particularly odious, and have been the occasion of bitter accusations against the Church.

With the exception of imprisonment, which we will speak of later on, these penalties originated with the State. It is important, therefore, to know what crimes they punished. As a general rule, it must be admitted that they were only inflicted upon those heretics who seriously disturbed the social order. If the death penalty could be justly meted out to such rioters, with still greater reason could the lesser penalties be inflicted.

The penalty of confiscation was especially cruel, inasmuch as it affected the posterity of the condemned heretics. According to the old Roman law, the property of heretics could be inherited by their orthodox sons, and even by their agnates and cognates.[2] The laws of the Middle Ages declared confiscation

[1] Lea, *op. cit.*, vol. i, p. 224.
[2] 4 and 19, cap *De hæreticis*, iv, 5, *Manichæos* and *Cognovimus*.

absolute; on the plea that heresy should be classed with treason, orthodox children could not inherit the property of their heretical father.[1] There was but one exception to this law. Frederic II and Innocent IV both decreed that children could inherit their father's property, if they denounced him for heresy.[2] It is needless to insist upon the odious character of such a law. We cannot understand to-day how Gregory IX could rejoice on learning that fathers did not scruple to denounce their children, children their parents, a wife her husband or a mother her children.[3]

Granting that banishment and confiscation were just penalties for heretics who were also State criminals, was it right for the Church to employ this penal system for the suppression of heresy alone?

It is certain that the early Christians would have strongly denounced such laws as too much like the pagan laws under which they were persecuted. St. Hilary voiced their mind when he said: "The Church threatens exile and imprisonment; she in whom men formerly believed while in exile and prison, now wishes to make men believe her by force."[4] St. Augustine was of the same mind. He thus addressed the Manicheans, the most hated sect of his time: "Let those who have never known the troubles of a mind in search for the truth, proceed against you with rigor. It is impossible for me to do so, for I for years was cruelly tossed about by your false doctrines, which I advocated

---

[1] Decretal *Vergentis* of Innocent III. Decretals, cap. x, *De Hæreticis*, lib. v, tit. vii.

[2] *Mon. Germ., Leges*, vol. ii, sect. iv, p. 197; Ripoll, *Bullarium ordinis Prædicat.*, vol. i, p. 126.

[3] Bull *Gaudemus*, of April 12, 1233, in Ripoll, vol. i, p. 56.

[4] *Liber contra Auxentium*, cap. iv; cf. *supra*, p. 6.

and defended to the best of my ability. I ought to bear with you now, as men bore with me, when I blindly accepted your doctrines."[1] Wazo, Bishop of Liège, wrote in a similar strain in the eleventh century.[2]

But, continued St. Augustine, retracting his first theory,—and nearly all the Middle Ages agreed with him,—"these severe penalties are lawful and good when they serve to convert heretics by inspiring them with a salutary fear." The end here justifies the means.

Such reasoning was calculated to lead men to great extremes, and was responsible for the cruel teaching of the theologians of the school, who were more logically consistent than the Bishop of Hippo. They endeavored to terrorize heretics by the specter of the stake. St. Augustine, bold as he was, shrank from such barbarity. But if, on his own admission, the logical consequences of the principle he laid down were to be rejected, did not this prove the principle itself false?

If we consider merely the immediate results obtained by the use of brute force, we may indeed admit that it benefited the Church by bringing back some of her erring children. But at the same time these cruel measures turned away from Catholicism in the course of ages many sensitive souls, who failed to recognize Christ's Church in a society which practiced such cruelty in union with the State. According, therefore,

---

[1] *Contra epistolam Manichæi, quam vocant Fundamenti*, n. 2 and 3, *supra*, p. 12.

[2] *Vita Vasonis*, cap. xxv and xxvi, Migne, P. L., vol. cxlii, col. 752, 753; cf. *supra*, p. 51.

to St. Augustine's own argument, his theory has been proved false by its fatal consequences.

We must, therefore, return to the first theory of St. Augustine, and be content to win heretics back to the true faith by purely moral constraint. The penalties, decreed or consented to by the Church, ought to be medicinal in character, viz., pilgrimages, flogging, wearing the crosses, and the like. Imprisonment may even be included in the list, for temporary imprisonment has a well-defined expiatory character. In fact that is why in the beginning the monasteries made it a punishment for heresy. If, later on, the Church frequently inflicted the penalty of life imprisonment, she did so because by a legal fiction she attributed to it a purely penitential character. Any one of these punishments, therefore, may be considered lawful, provided it is not arbitrarily inflicted. This theory does not permit the Church to abandon impenitent heretics to the secular arm. It grants her only the right of excommunication, according to the penitential discipline and the primitive canon law of the days of Tertullian, Cyprian, Origen, Lactantius, and Hilary.

. . . .

But is this return to antiquity conformable to the spirit of the Church? Can it be reconciled in particular with one of the condemned propositions of the Syllabus: *Ecclesia vis inferendæ potestatem non habet*?[1] *The Church has no right to use force.*

Without discussing this proposition at length, let us first state that authorities are not agreed on its precise meaning. Every Catholic will admit that the Church has a coercive power, in both the external and the in-

[1] Proposit, xxiv.

ternal forum. But the question under dispute—and this the Syllabus does not touch—is whether the coercive power comprises merely spiritual penalties, or temporal and corporal penalties as well. The editor of the Syllabus did not decide this question; he merely, referred us to the letter *Ad Apostolicæ Sedis* of August 22, 1851. But this letter is not at all explicit; it merely condemns those who pretend " to deprive the Church of the external jurisdiction and coercive power which was given her to win back sinners to the ways of righteousness." We would like to find more light on this question elsewhere. But the theologians who at the Vatican Council prepared canons 10 and 12 of the schema *De Ecclesia* on this very point of doctrine did not remove the ambiguity. They explicitly affirmed that the Church had the right to exercise over her erring children " constraint by an external judgment and salutary penalties," but they said nothing about the nature of these penalties. Was not such silence significant? It authorized, one may safely say, the opinion of those who limited the coercive power of the Church to merely moral constrain.. Cardinal Soglia, in a work approved by Gregory XVI and Pius IX, declared that this opinion was " more in harmony with the gentleness of the Church." [1] It also has in its favor Popes Nicholas I [2] and Celestine III,[3] who

[1] *Institutiones juris publici ecclesiastici*, 5 ed., Paris, vol. i, pp. 169, 170.

[2] *Nicolai, Ep.* ad Albinum archiepiscop., in the *Decretum*, Causa xxxiii, quæst. ii, cap. *Inter hæc.*

[3] Celestine, according to the criminal code of his day, declared that a guilty cleric, once excommunicated and anathematized, ought to be abandoned to the secular arm, *cum Ecclesia non habeat ultra quid faciat.* Decretals, cap. x, *De judiciis*, lib. ii, tit. i. This was the common teaching.

claimed for the Church of which they were the head the right to use only the spiritual sword. Without enumerating all the modern authors who hold this view, we will quote a work which has just appeared with the *imprimatur* of Father Lepidi, the Master of the Sacred Palace, in which we find the two following theses proved: 1. " Constraint, in the sense of employing violence to enforce ecclesiastical laws, originated with the State." 2. "The constraint of ecclesiastical laws is by divine right exclusively moral constraint." [1]

Indeed, to maintain that the Church should use material force, is at once to make her subject to the State; for we can hardly picture her with her own police and gendarmes, ready to punish her rebellious children. Every Catholic believes that the Church is an independent society, fully able to carry out her divine mission without the aid of the secular arm Whether governments are favorable or hostile to her, she must pursue her course and carry on her work of salvation under them all.

. . . .

" Heresy," writes Jean Guiraud, " in the Middle Ages was nearly always connected with some antisocial sect. In a period when the human mind usually expressed itself in a theological form, socialism, communism, and anarchy appeared under the form of heresy. By the very nature of things, therefore, the

---

[1] Salvatore di Bartolo. *Nuova espozitione dei criteri teologici*, Roma, 1904, pp. 303, 314. The first edition of this work was put upon the Index. The second edition, revised and corrected, and published with the approbation of Father Lepidi, has all the more weight and authority.

interests of both Church and State were identical; this explains the question of the suppression of heresy in the Middle Ages." [1]

We are not surprised, therefore, that when Church and State found themselves menaced by the same peril, they agreed on the means of defence. If we deduct from the total number of heretics burned or imprisoned the disturbers of the social order and the criminals against the common law, the number of condemned heretics will be very small.

Heretics in the Middle Ages were considered amenable to the laws of both Church and State. Men of that time could not conceive of God and His revelation without defenders in a Christian kingdom. Magistrates were considered responsible for the sins committed against the law of God. Indirectly, therefore, heresy was amenable to their tribunal. They felt it their right and duty to punish not only crimes against society, but sins against faith.

The Inquisition, established to judge heretics, is, therefore, an institution whose severity and cruelty are explained by the ideas and manners of the age. We will never understand it, unless we consider it in its environment, and from the viewpoint of men like St. Thomas Aquinas and St. Louis, who dominated their age by their genius. Critics who are ignorant of the Middle Ages may feel at liberty to shower insult and contempt upon a judicial system whose severity is naturally repugnant to them. But contempt does not always imply a reasonable judgment, and to abuse an institution is not necessarily a proof

[1] Jean Guiraud, *La répression de l'hérésie au moyen âge*, in the *Questions d'archéologie et d'histoire*, p. 44.

of intelligence. If we would judge an epoch intelligently, we must be able to grasp the viewpoint of other men, even if they lived in an age long past.

But although we grant the good faith and good will of the founders and judges of the Inquisition—we speak only, be it understood, of those who acted conscientiously—we must still maintain that their idea of justice was far inferior to ours. Whether taken in itself or compared with other criminal procedures, the Inquisition was, so far as the guarantees of equity are concerned, undoubtedly unjust and inferior. Such judicial forms as the secrecy of the trial, the prosecution carried on independently of the prisoner, the denial of advocate and defence, the use of torture, etc., were certainly despotic and barbarous. Severe penalties, like the stake and confiscation, were the legacy which a pagan legislation bequeathed to the Christian State; they were alien to the spirit of the Gospel.

The Church in a measure felt this, for to enforce these laws she always had recourse to the secular arm. In time, all this criminal code was to fall into desuetude, and no one to-day wishes it back again. Besides, the crying abuses committed by some of the Inquisitors have made the institution forever odious.

But in abandoning the system of force, which she formerly used in union with the State, does not the Church seem to condemn, to a certain degree, her past?

Even if to-day she were to denounce the Inquisition, she would not thereby compromise her divine authority. Her office on earth is to transmit to generation after generation the deposit of revealed truths necessary for man's salvation. That to safeguard this treasure she uses means in one age which a later age denounces, merely proves that she follows the customs and ideas in vogue around her. But she takes good care not to have men consider her attitude the infallible and eternal rule of absolute justice. She readily admits that she may sometimes be deceived in the choice of means of government. The system of defence and protection that she adopted in the Middle Ages succeeded, at least to some extent. We cannot maintain that it was absolutely unjust and absolutely immoral.

Undoubtedly we have to-day a much higher ideal of justice. But though we deplore the fact that the Church did not then perceive, preach or apply it, we need not be surprised. In social questions she ordinarily progresses with the march of civilization, of which she is ever one of the prime movers.

But perhaps men may blame her for having abandoned and betrayed the cause of toleration, which she so ably defended in the beginning. Do not let us exaggerate. There was, undoubtedly, a period in which she did not deduce, from the principle she was the first to teach, all its logical consequences. The laws she enforced against heretics prove this. But it is false to say that, while in the beginning she insisted strongly on the rights of conscience, she afterwards totally disregarded them. In fact, she exercised constraint only over her own stray children. But while she acted so cruelly toward them, she never ceased to respect the consciences of those outside her fold. She always interpreted the *compelle intrare* to imply with regard to unbelievers moral constraint, and the means of gentleness and persuasion. If respect for human liberty is to-day dominant in the thinking world, it is due chiefly to her.

In the matter of tolerance, the Church has only to study her own history. If, during several centuries, she treated her rebellious children with greater severity than those alien to her fold, it was not from a want of consistency. And if to-day she manifests to every one signs of her maternal kindness, and lays aside for ever all physical constraint, she is not following the example of non-Catholics, but merely taking up again the interrupted tradition of her early Fathers.

INDEX

Abjuration, 92
Abrenuntiatio of the Cathari, 61
Absolution, mutual of Inquisitors, 110
Accusatio, 120
Adalbero, Bishop of Liège, on tolerance of, 29
Adam, trial of, 121
Ad Extirpanda, the bull, 104, 108, 109
Adoptianism, 24
Adrian IV, and Arnold of Brescia, 30
Advocates, denied by Inquisition, 89
Alba, Cathari of, 51
Albertus Magnus, and witchcraft, 118
Albigenses, crusade against, 45
Alexander III, his laws against heresy, 42, 43
Alexander IV, and torture, 108, 110
on testimony of heretics, 89
Alexis Comnenus, 50
Amaury de Beynes, 41
Ambrose, St., denounces the condemnation of Priscillian, 20
Animadversio, various meanings of, 43, 45, 75, 76, 79, 94, 126, 128

Annibale, Senator of Rome, 79
Anselm of Lucca, 47
Apparellamentum, of the Cathari, 65
Apringius, 14
Arcadius, law against heretics, 154
Arnold of Brescia, 30
Augustine, St., his toleration, 9
and the Donatists, 12–16
his denunciation of Priscillianism, 20
Auto-da-fé, 99, 141, 150

Bagolenses, 52
Ban, the imperial, 43, 76
Banishment, for heresy, 43, 48, 123, 126, 154
Baptism, rejected by Cathari, 54
Benencasa, 48
Bernard, St., on toleration, 34
opposes Arnold of Brescia, 30
Bernard, St., opposes Henry of Lausanne, 30
Bernard of Caux, his treatment of the relapsed, 126
his sentences, 140
Bernard of Como, on the witches' Sabbat, 119

INDEX

Bernard Gui, and the Inquisitorial procedure, 120
  approves of torture, 112
  his sentences, 141
Bléda, and the banishment of the Moriscos, 145
Bogomiles, 50
Bonacursus, 51
Boniface VIII, 98, 168
Braisne, Cathari burned at, 41
Bread, blessed of Cathari, 64
Bullinger approves of death penalty for heresy, 163

Cæsarius of Heisterbach, on the number of the Cathari, 51
Calixtus II, 36.
Calvin, advocates death penalty, 163
Cambrai, heretic burned at, 27
Capital punishment, denied by Cathari, 57
Cathari, different names of, 52
  fasting of, 65
  hierarchy of, 58
  number of, 51
  their teachings, 52 *et seq.*
Celestine III, 183
Celibacy, Catharan idea of, 66–70
  Catholic idea of, 74
Châlons, Cathari at, 26
Charles II (England), 162
Chrysostom, St., on toleration, 22
Circumcelliones, 8, 11
Clement IV, and torture, 108
  and the episcopal Inquisition, 98

Clement IV, enforces bull *Ad Extirpanda*, 105
  on the number of witnesses, 88
Clement V, and the Templars, 136
  and prison reform, 103
  on the cruelty of Inquisitors, 135
Coals, torture of the burning, 110
Cologne, heretics burned at, 29, 40
Concorrezenses, 52
Confiscation, 42, 44, 48, 123, 126, 147–149
Conrad of Marburg, 82, 87, 93
Consolamentum, 54, 59, 60
Constantine the Great, 4, 53
Convenenza, 59
Council of Rome (313), 11,
  of Arles (314), 11
  of Mainz (848), 25
  of Quierzy (849), 25
  of Rheims (1049), 36
  of Toulouse (1119), 36, 66
  of Rheims (1148), 31
  of Tours (1163), 41, 42
  of Verona (1184), 103
  of Avignon (1209), 39, 48
  of Lateran (1215), 45, 76
  of Narbonne (1227), 84
  of Toulouse (1229), 76, 102
Cyprian, St., on toleration, 3

Decretals, respect due to the, 117
De hæretico comburendo, 161, 162
Demons, *succubi* and *incubi*, 146
Denunciation, duty of, 88
Denuntiatio, 120
Dominicans, as Inquisitors, 85
Donatists, 10 *et seq.*

INDEX

Edict of Milan, 4
Edward VI (England), 161
Elipandus, 24
Elizabeth (England), 162
Endura, 70–72
Éon de l'Étoile, 31
Eriberto, 28
Eugenius III, 47, 31
Evervin, 34
Evodius, 18
Excommunication of abettors of heresy, 44, 104, 105
of heretics, 123
Exhumation, of dead heretics, 148
Experts, for heresy trials, 99
assembly of, 99–101
Eymeric, and the Inquisitorial procedure, 120
on torture, 121
picture of ideal Inquisitor, 113

Farel, approves of death-penalty, 162
Fasts of the Cathari, 65
Felix of Urgel, 24
Flogging, 13, 106, 108
Franciscans, as Inquisitors, 85
Frederic II (Emperor), his legislation against heresy, 77, 89, 94, 95, 173
his influence upon Gregory IX, 80
uses Inquisition for political ends, 136

Geroch of Reichersberg, 34, 37
Godescalcus, on predestination, 25
Goslar, heretics hanged at, 27

Grace, time of, 88
Gratian, 39, 47, 106
Gregory IX, and torture, 107
his laws against ordeals, 107
his legislation against heresy, 78, 81, 94
institutes the Inquisition, 81, 83
Gregory X, and the Episcopal Inquisition, 98
Guala, Bishop of Brescia, 77, 78
Gui Foucois, cf. Clement IV
Guibert de Nogent, 29
Guillaume, Archbishop of Rheims, 40
Guiraud, 184

Henry III (Emperor), 27
Henry V (England), 161
Henry VIII (England), 161
Henry of Lausanne, 30
Henry of Milan, 81
Henry of Susa, 128
Heresy, a political factor, 136
a public crime, 173
considered treason, 77, 80
definitions of, 116
of the Cathari, 52 *et seq.*
relapse into, 126, 127
Heretication, 56, 58, 59, 60, 68, 154
Hilary, St., on toleration, 5
Hincmar, Archbishop of Rheims, 25
Honorius III, his legislation against heretics, 77
his law against ordeals, 107
Honorius IV, 132
Hugh, Bishop of Auxerre, 40
Huguccio, advocates death-penalty, 47
Humiliati, 45
Huss, 164

Idacius, 18
Imprisonment, antecedent, 108, 169
 character of, 102, 137, 138, 142
 for relapse, 237
 purpose of, 37
Innocent III, and the Patarins, 115
 classes heresy with treason, 45
 does not inflict death penalty, 46
 his laws against ordeals, 107
 his legislation on heresy, 43–46
 his treatment of Raymond VI, 46
Innocent IV, and the episcopal Inquisition, 98
 authorizes torture, 105, 107
 his legislation against heresy, 104, 108, 110
Innocent VIII, his bull on sorcery, 146
In pace, 140
Inquisitor, aged required, 93
 cruelty of, 134, 135
 duties of, 87
 portrait of, 93
Inquisitio, 120
Inquisition, development of, 86 *et seq.*
 its origin, 81, 83
 its spread, 132 *et seq.*
 number of victims of, 172
 political use of, 136
 procedure of, 167
 the episcopal, 83, 97
 the legatine, 85
 used against Joan of Arc, 137
 used to crush the Templars, 136

Intolerance, natural to man, 155
 of Plato, 156
 of sovereigns, 156
Irregularity, incurred by Inquisitors, 110
Isidore, St., of Seville, 23
Ithacius, 18
Ivo of Chartres, 47

Jailers, rules for, 138
Jean Galand, 134
Jeanne de la Tour, 139
Jean d'André, 128
Jerome, St., denounces Priscillianism, 20
 his idea of schism, 116
Jews, and usury, 118
 banished from Spain, 145
Joan of Arc, 137
John Teutonicus, 47
Justinian, code of, 47

Kiss, Catharan, of peace, 63

Lactantius, on toleration, 4
Lateran, cf. Council.
Lea, admits the small number of victims, 150
 estimate of his history, vi
Leo, St., the Great, and the Priscillianists, 21
 on persecution, 21
Leo IX, 36
Lollardy, 161
Louis VIII (France), 75
Louis IX, St. (France), 75
Lucas, Bishop of Tuy, 85
Lucius III, his legislation against heresy, 43, 103
 his decretal *ad Abolendam*, 126
 regulates the episcopal Inquisition, 83

INDEX

Magic, accusation against Priscillain, 19
  considered heresy, 118
Maistre, Joseph de, 176
Malleus Maleficarum, 130, 146
Manicheans, persecution of, 9, 10
  law of Diocletian against, 8
Marriage, denounced by Cathari, 66 *et seq.*
Marsollier, Jacques, vi, 110
Martin, St., his tolerance, 18
Martin V, and usurers, 118
Maximus (Emperor), 18
Metempsychosis, of the Cathari, 66
Milan, heretics burned at, 28, 81
Molay, Jacques, 136
Monteforte, heretics burned at, 28
Mont-Wimer, heretics burned at, 82
Moranis, 133
Moriscos, 145

Names, of witnesses withheld, 90
Newman, Cardinal, on suppression of facts, viii
Nevers, heretics burned at, 41
Nicholas I, denounces the use of torture, 106, 170
  on ecclesiastical penalties, 187
Nicholas IV, his legislation against heresy, 105

Oath, use of, denounced by the Cathari, 56
Optatus, St., advocates the death penalty, 11
Ordeals, 91, 106

Origen, tolerance of, 3
Orleans, heretics burned at, 26

Pamiers, registers of, 141, 143
Panormia, 47
Paramo, 121, 146
Paris, heretics burned at, 41
Pastor, on Innocent VIII, 146
Patarins, 52
Patricius, 19
Paul, St., excommunicates heretics, 1
Paulicians, massacre of, 50
Peter of Bruys, 29
Peter Cantor, 34, 37, 178
Peter, St., of Verona, 81
Pierre Cauchon, 137
Pierre Mauran, 41
Philip Augustus, 41
Philip, Count of Flanders, 40
Philip the Fair, 134, 136
Pilgrimages, as penances, 88
Plato, 156
Prayer, the Lord's, 61
Primacy, of the Pope, denied by the Cathari, 53
Priscillianism, 17–21
Probatio of the Cathari, 62

Rack, torture of, 109
Raymond V, 41
Raymond, St., of Pennafort, 116–123
Relapse, penalty for, 126, 127, 155, 174
Responsibility of the Church in the infliction of the death penalty, 31, 32, 37, 103 *et seq.*, 128 *et seq.*
Ritual, of the Cathari, 61, 62
Robert the Bougre, 133
Robert the Pious, 26

Roman law, revival of, 39, 107
Rome, Patarins, burned in, 79

Sabbat, the witches', 118
Sacraments, denied by the Cathari, 54
Sardinia, inquisition in, 132
  Cathari in, 28
Savonarola, 135
Secrecy of the Inquisition, 121.
Secular arm, abandonment to the, 43, 48, 92, 127, 129, 143
Sermo generalis, 99, 141, 150
Servetus, 163
Sicilian Code, of Frederic II, 80, 81, 107, 115, 154, 158
Simon de Montfort, 42
Soglia, Cardinal, theory of toleration, 183
Soissons, heretics burned at, 28
Sophronisteria, 156
Spain, Inquisition in, 137, 144, 145
Speronistæ, 52
Sprenger, 130, 146
Stake, penalty of the, 24, 27, 28, 29, 40, 41, 43, 45, 46, 77, 81, 82, 92, 94, 143, 144, 174
Strasburg, heretics burned at, 78
Suger, Abbot, 31
Sulpicius Severus, 20
Superstition, classed as heresy, 117
Syllabus, the, 182
Synodal witnesses, 84

Talio, penalty of the, 120
Taxation, its lawfulness denied by the Cathari, 56

Templars, 136
Tertullian, on toleration, 2, 3
Theodora, the Empress, 50
Theodore of Beza, 164
Theodosius I (Emperor), 7
Theodosius II (Emperor), 7
Theodwin of Liège, 33
Theognitus, 22
Thomas Aquinas, St., definition of heresy, 116
  defends the death penalty, 123 *et seq.*
  on the relapsed, 126, 173
Torquemada, 144, 145
Torture, condemned by Nicholas I, 106, 170
  different forms of, 108–110
  in the trials of the Inquisition, 106–114, 169
  length of, 111
  of witnesses, 122
  presence of clerics at, 110
  recommended by Bernard Gui, 112
  repetition of, 121
  value of confessions, extorted by, 111
Transmigration, of souls, 60

Urban IV, and the episcopal Inquisition, 98
  and the Inquisitorial procedure, 120
  and torture, 111
Usury, 118

Valentinian I, 7
Veneration of Cathari, 59
Verona, heretics burned at, 81
Veronese code, 107
Vestment, sacred, of the Cathari, 63
Vezelai, heretics burned at, 40

INDEX

Vilgard, 27
Viterbo, Paterins at, 45

War denounced by Cathari, 57
Wazo, of Liège, 33
Witchcraft, 146, 147
Witnesses, character of, 88
  dangers incurred by, 90
Witnesses, few for the defence, 89
  number required, 88
  refused for enmity, 89
  Synodal, 84
Wyclif, 160

Zanchino Ugolino, 117
Zurkinden, 164

www.ingramcontent.com/pod-product-compliance
Lightning Source LLC
Chambersburg PA
CBHW022006100426
42738CB00041B/330